Luminous Construction

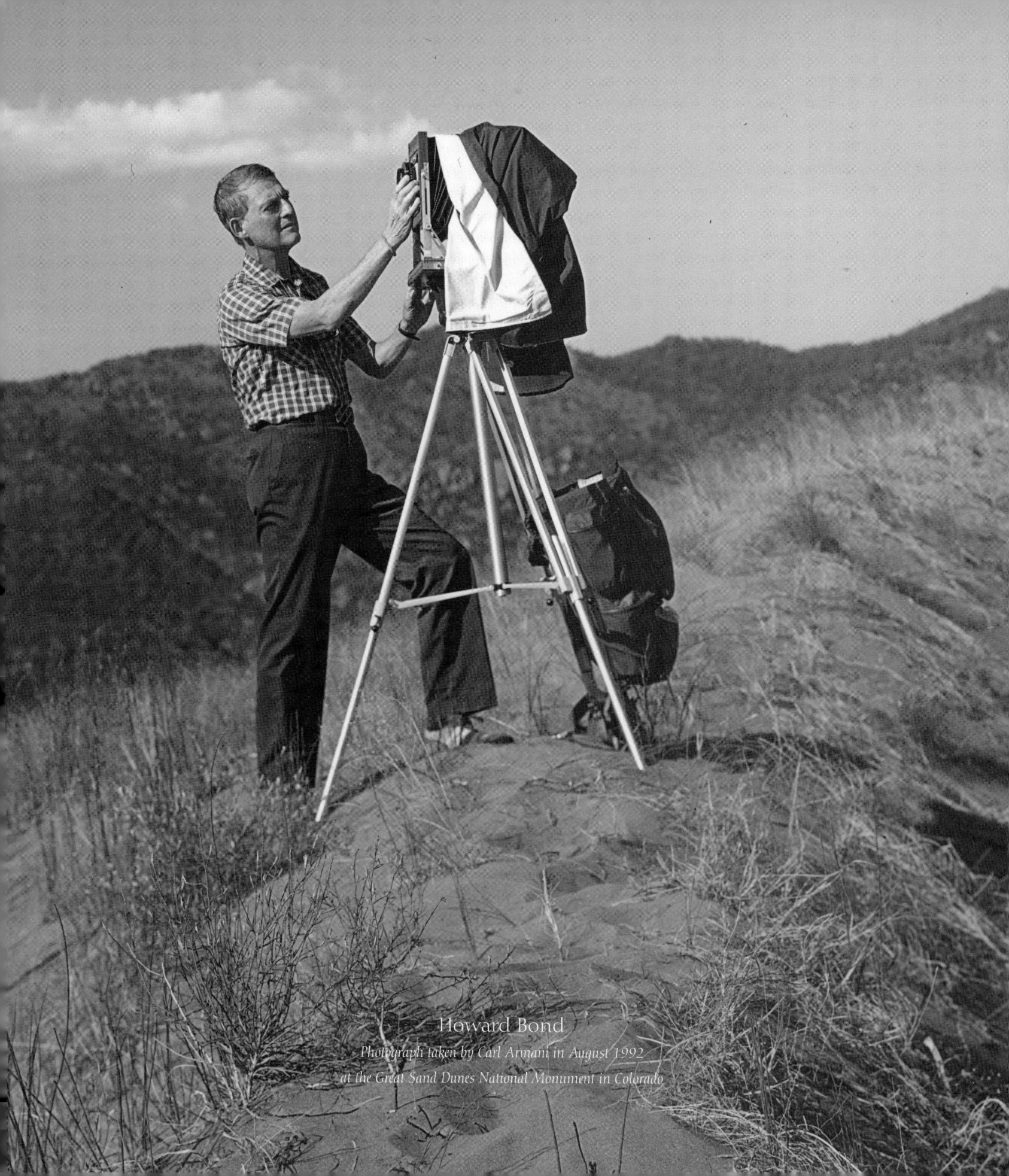

Howard Bond
Photograph taken by Carl Armani in August 1992
at the Great Sand Dunes National Monument in Colorado

Luminous Construction

The Photography of

HOWARD BOND

An exhibition held at the Special Collections Research Center
between 8 September 2009 and 14 January 2010.
Support for this catalog came from Carl J. and Marcy Armani.

Foreword

In 1917, two young cousins in Cottingley, England, photographed fairies—or so they claimed. Noted author and spiritualist Sir Arthur Conan Doyle was among those who believed that the black-and-white prints, in which fairies fluttered about with the girls in a garden, were authentic. What I find so interesting about this story is that Elsie Wright, sixteen, and Frances Griffiths, ten, claimed that they were clairvoyant, and that the camera had simply enabled others to see what they had seen. The existence of the fairy world, long suspected to be real, albeit just beyond most people's perception, had been confirmed by the powers of technology.

Of course, the Cottingley fairies turned out to be a hoax. Elsie and Frances had contrived the appearance of winged creatures in the photos. Nevertheless, their canard prompts us to consider some fundamental questions about photography. On some level, isn't all photography about revealing fairies, that is, the overlooked wonder of real-world things? Are great photographers able to see more deeply than the rest of us? Or are they simply technicians who are able to fool us? What does the language we choose to describe photography reveal about our feelings towards it? Do we "take" photographs or "capture" them?

Howard Bond says that he "constructs" photographs. In his preface to *White Motif* (1990), one of his two published volumes, Bond explains: "I wanted to *construct* images by manipulating shapes on the ground glass, using the view camera adjustments. The whitewashed buildings, along with the shadows and textures formed by the Mediterranean sun, would be the raw materials for my designs. Filtered blue skies could provide black accents. The prints, achieved by ordinary straight photographic means, might be more abstractions than records." To extend the metaphor, Bond is a kind of architect, manipulating light, texture, and tonality instead of bricks, mortar, and steel.

Bond's tool of choice is the large-format or view camera, which has changed little since the mid-nineteenth century. The camera is comprised of two planes connected by accordion-like bellows. The image is composed first on a ground-glass plate and then transferred directly onto a large film sheet. The camera sits on a tripod and the photographer adjusts it on horizontal and vertical planes in an effort to perfect the resulting image. View cameras are cumbersome, and the very act of constructing an image requires both physical endurance and intellectual discipline.

Bond was born in Napoleon, Ohio, in 1931. He holds a bachelor's degree in music from Bowling Green University (1953) and master's degrees in music (1958) and mathematics (1961) from the University of Michigan, Ann Arbor. In addition to a five-year stint as a music teacher, he was employed as a computer programmer with General Motors, Bendix, the University of Michigan, and Horiba Instruments. A photographer from the age of fourteen, he enrolled as an adult in workshops taught by Ansel Adams, Imogen Cunningham, and Brett Weston. He committed himself full-time to photography in 1979.

Each of his twenty-two portfolios reflects his perambulations to far-flung and widely varying locations such as Austria, England, Greece, Ontario, the American West, and the junkyards of the American upper Midwest. His subjects range from open landscapes, as in "Light Triangle" (1991), to abstract details, as in "Bristlecone Pine No. 2, Colorado" (1993). Though Bond has tended to favor inanimate subjects, his few portraits are arresting; and they are landscapes in their own right. For example, the furrowed face of the ninety-three-year-old widow Kyriako from the Greek islands blends into weathered shutters and a cracked plaster windowsill.

The paucity of portraits in Bond's oeuvre may reflect not a lack of interest in humanity, but rather, his deep respect for it. In the preface to *White Motif* he recalls meeting Kyriako: "Though we couldn't communicate verbally, we had a fine time, and she gave me a large cucumber before parting. The next year, I was very fortunate to find her youngest son visiting her for the first time since immigrating to Australia twenty-eight years earlier. From him I learned her age, that her husband had been killed near the end of World War II, and that she had six children. Finally, I knew how many prints to send!"

In addition to Syracuse University Library, Howard Bond's photographs can be found in the collections of the Bibliothèque Nationale, the Victoria and Albert Museum, the Art Institute of Chicago, Harvard University's Fogg Museum, the San Francisco Museum of Modern Art, and the Library of Congress. Museums and galleries from Amarillo to Athens have staged one-man exhibitions of his work.

A complete set of his twenty-two portfolios came to Syracuse University in 2008, the gift of Carl J. Armani '60 and his wife, Marcy. At Syracuse University Library, Howard Bond's portfolios reside with the photographs of Margaret Bourke White (1904–1971), Clara E. Sipprell (1885–1975), Louis Fabian Bachrach (1881–1963), Victor Keppler

(1904–1987), and Ewing Galloway (1881–1953). Other sympathetic neighbors of the Bond portfolios include the papers of sculptors Anna Hyatt Huntington (1876–1973) and James Earl Fraser (1876–1953), as well as watercolorist Frederic Whitaker (1891–1980), whose work celebrates the wildness of the American West.

Dean Suzanne Thorin and I are grateful for Carl and Marcy Armani's generous gift to Syracuse, which will inspire generations of students. We owe a debt of gratitude to the lead curator, Kelli Pennington G '10, a master of fine arts photography student. She brings to this exhibition an intense eye, tempered by a deep respect for those who have mastered the craft of photography. Kelli encourages us to see the images more deeply by recontextualizing Bond's work through the categories of proximity, texture, pattern, abstraction, and place.

Like Elsie and Francis of Cottingley, England, the photographer seeks to show us something that might not otherwise be seen. It could be the texture of an old woman's cheek, or a cathedral's straining skeleton, or a gnarled knot of pine. I invite you to look carefully at the photographs of Howard Bond. Who knows what you might find?

Sean Quimby
Director of Special Collections
Syracuse University Library

How the Portfolios of Howard Bond Found a Home at Syracuse University

I spent my early years in Syracuse, New York, during an age that predated television, computers, DVDs, and digital cameras. My windows to the broader world were photography, the written word, radio, and movies. For me, *Life* magazine, with its vivid photographic essays, was a source of adventure and learning. I fell in love with the photograph—nothing more than light on paper—and my most valued possessions were a Kodak Brownie camera, film, flash bulbs, and the crude darkroom I constructed in the basement of my family's home.

Three decades later I moved on to large-format cameras. I was an amateur "shutterbug," hoping to create fine art. With a passion approaching obsession, I read every available book on technique and studied the lives and works of the great masters Ansel Adams, Edward Weston, Alfred Stieglitz, and Edward Steichen. Alas, my first attempts at large-format photography were not very successful.

I decided that I needed help, so I asked a friend who owned a local photography gallery to recommend a workshop. He immediately suggested one offered by Howard Bond that was conducted in Ann Arbor, Michigan. In late 1982, I flew to Michigan from my home in Denver, Colorado, to attend his weekend workshop on the zone system and on large-format camera techniques.

Howard was an excellent teacher. His teaching method was based on science, humor, common sense, and an ability to communicate a developed tonal vision. When we passed our own prints around, we found his critiques to be kind and generous, without a hint of degrading sarcasm. He would print students' negatives in his dark-room and create wonderful pictures with broad tonal ranges. We students often asked, "Why can't I get the same quality out of that negative?" The answer is that, while all photographers have the same tools available to them, what sets the great photographers apart is their complete understanding of their medium and their ability to see form, light, and shadow. Howard is a master of his medium. His photographs are sharply focused, detailed, and exquisitely lit.

I returned to Denver with a new confidence in my ability as a photographer and a printmaker, and the desire to own some of Howard Bond's photographs. Soon thereafter, I started to buy Howard's work directly from him and from a local gallery. First, I purchased individual prints and, later, entire portfolios. After I had acquired fifteen individual prints and ten portfolios, I decided that over time I would purchase every portfolio he ever produced. Howard always kept his prices reasonable so that his work would be accessible. He generously helped me to fill the gaps in my collection. When Howard released *Portfolio XXII: Aegean Light* in 2005, he said that it would be his last. After twenty-six years of collecting, I had acquired all twenty-two portfolios and thirty single images of various sizes.

After I decided to donate all the portfolios to a museum or a university, I searched for three years to find a home for my collection. My short list included several western museums and my alma mater, Syracuse University. In September 2007, my wife, Marcy, and I attended a fraternity reunion there. Even though Syracuse was my hometown, this was my first visit to campus since I graduated in 1960. I was so happy to see the beautiful campus and the faces of the young students who were embarking on one of the greatest adventures of their lives. As we left the campus, Marcy looked at me and said, "This is where your beautiful collection belongs. This is your hometown and this university helped to mold you." I knew immediately that she was right; Syracuse University and the city of Syracuse was my first and only choice.

I started corresponding with Sean Quimby, director of the Special Collections Research Center in Bird Library. Sean and I discussed the library's collecting needs and policies and my desires for the disposition and use of the collection. In August 2008 on a visit to the university, I conferred with him personally. In September 2008, he flew to Denver and we spent two days browsing the collection. We worked out the details of the gift agreement by e-mail and telephone, and in December 2008, I shipped the twenty-two portfolios.

I listed three main conditions for the gift: it must be exhibited; made available for loan to other museums and educational institutions; and accessible to students, faculty, and members of the public wishing not only to view, but also to handle the prints. I have always felt that to establish a personal relationship with art one should physically interact with it. The Special Collections Research Center aspires to be a "laboratory" where modern hands can explore "the artifacts of history." That mission matched my goals perfectly.

I will leave to others the task of describing Howard's work. Here I will say a few words about the man himself. Over the years, Marcy and I have become personal friends with Howard and Margaret Bond. We know him to be a humble, kind, generous, and talented man. He has lived his passion, through writing, teaching, and, most importantly, making photographs. At the confluence of heart, mind, and experience lies creative vision. Howard's vision has been fine-tuned by traveling the world with his large-format camera, often in physically challenging conditions. His landscapes are vast and small; he embraces the discarded and the new. For more than fifty years, enthusiasm, skill, and creativity have fueled his image-quest.

Oliver Wendell Holmes wrote: "A few can touch the magic string / And noisy Fame is proud to win them / Alas for those that never sing / But die with all their music in them!" Howard Bond will leave hundreds of photographic works of art, beautifully conceived and executed, for all to see and be inspired by.

Carl Armani
Syracuse University Class of 1960

Preface

Since its inception, photography has vied for a position among the "high" arts. Some theorists maintain that the works of formalist photographers such as Ansel Adams and Brett Weston—and, I would argue, their student Howard Bond—have helped photography attain that status.

Formalist photography places more emphasis on the esthetic value of a photograph than on its role as a document or record. In the introduction to his twenty-second and final portfolio, Bond writes, "Not infrequently, I have been more interested in creating simple, strong designs than in simply documenting the appearance of what was before my camera."

Formalist photographers resist narrative, focusing instead on design elements such as line, shape, texture, and pattern. When these design elements are combined with the elements of photography, including vantage point, frame, time, and detail, the resulting images render the world on a purely esthetic level.

Howard Bond has traveled to ten countries in search of subjects. Between 1974 and 2005 he released twenty-two portfolios of about ten photographs each, and he created some thirty sets of each portfolio. These portfolios reach across time, pulling images from different journeys together around unifying themes. His works are rich with precise detail. The world we see through his lens is a peaceful one, changed only by light and time.

Like most formalist photographers, Bond works with large-format cameras. Though cumbersome and complicated, these cameras allow photographers to have enhanced control over perspective and depth of field. To obtain his images, Bond transported his camera, tripod, lenses, and film holders to chosen sites, including mountainsides and streams. After placing the camera on the tripod and aiming the lens toward a subject, he stood under a dark cloth, twisting and turning the lens board and the the film plane to obtain optimal focus while assessing the inverted image on the ground glass.

He then metered the light and dark areas of the subject. This indicated the correct exposure and also whether or not the subject had a normal brightness range. If greater than normal, he could plan for less development than usual and, if less than normal, more development, so that the resulting negative would be suitable for a wide variety of interpretations at the printing stage.

With the film holder placed in its slot at the rear of the camera, in the position formerly occupied by the ground glass, the exposure could be made. The setup and exposure process took about fifteen minutes after he decided exactly what should be included in the photograph, if no waiting for ideal light was required. Later, he spent many hours in the darkroom, perfecting his prints.

In a telephone conversation with Howard Bond, I shared with him my selection process. Though I used some of his themes, such as abstraction and proximity, my interpretation of his work resulted in different groupings. He replied, "I'm intrigued. After I finished with a portfolio, I didn't often look back."

Now we as viewers can do the looking back. In the following pages, one can experience Bond's photographs in a context intended to foreground his achievement as a formalist, a craftsman, and an artist.

Kelli Pennington, Lead Curator
Master of Fine Arts Photography Student
Syracuse University

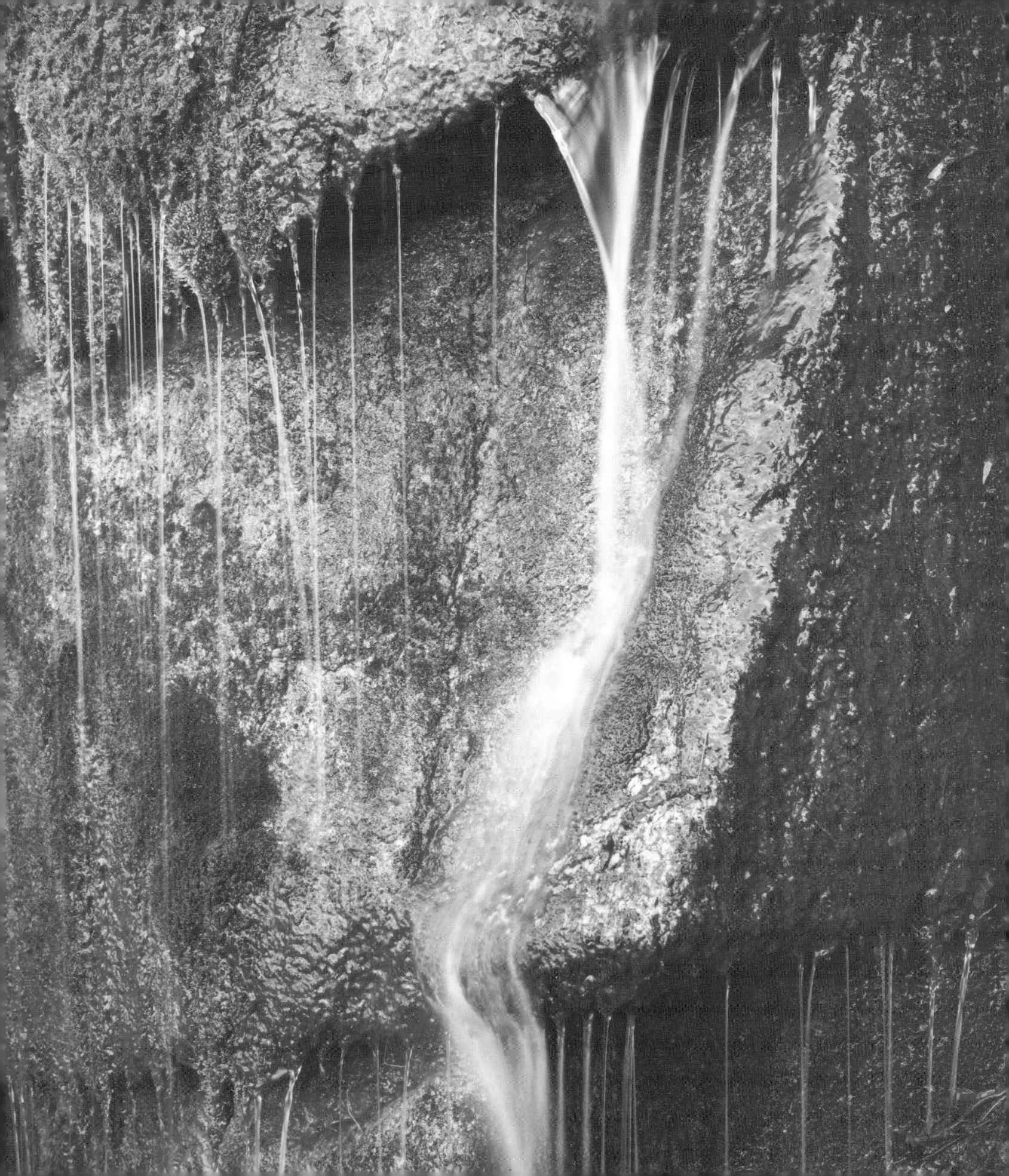

Proximity

Each photograph reveals a fraction of the world. In his *Portfolio VII: Proximity*, Bond states that the photographs "have in common nearness of the camera to the subject." He writes, "This tendency to move in close and include less than the whole is consistent with my attitude toward the relationship between subject and image. To me the subject is raw material from which to construct an image, rather than something to document. As a result, the important thing is not in front of the camera, but rather, what I can make of it."

In fact, Bond alternates between close-ups—so close that the resulting photograph is abstracted from its original context—and vast landscapes. He has mastered the interplay of subject and proximity to the camera lens, providing well-composed images no matter the distance.

"Brothers and Sister, Kuala Lumpur, Malaysia" (1973), one of Bond's few photographs of people, shows two brothers and their sister looking straight into the camera lens. The oldest child, in the middle, clutches the hands of his siblings, protecting them. Bond's camera is close, but not intrusively close; the frame allows the viewer space, unobstructed by building or street details, to infer the intricacies of the relationships.

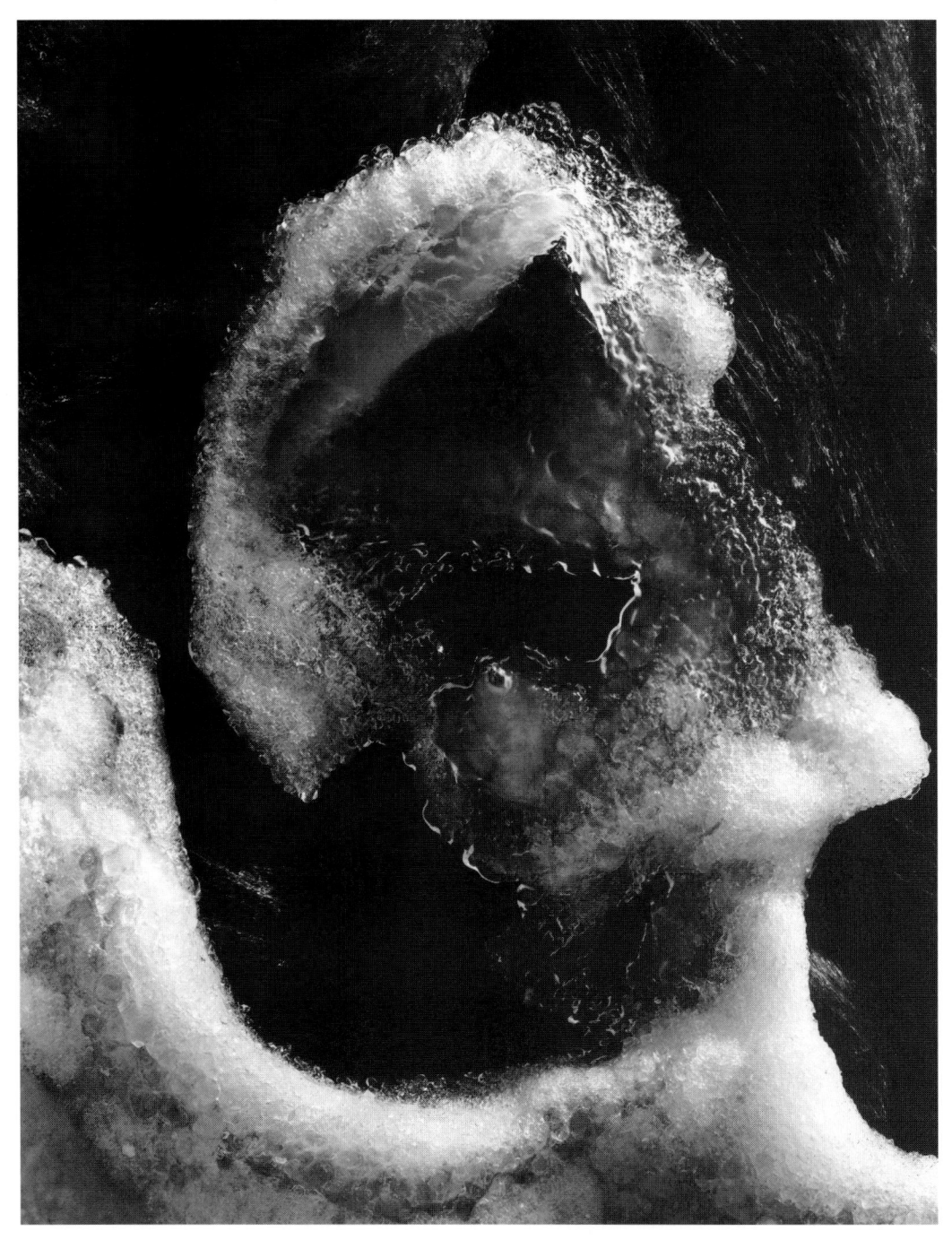

"Ice Detail No. 3," 1974

Silver gelatin print, *Portfolio IV: Huron River*

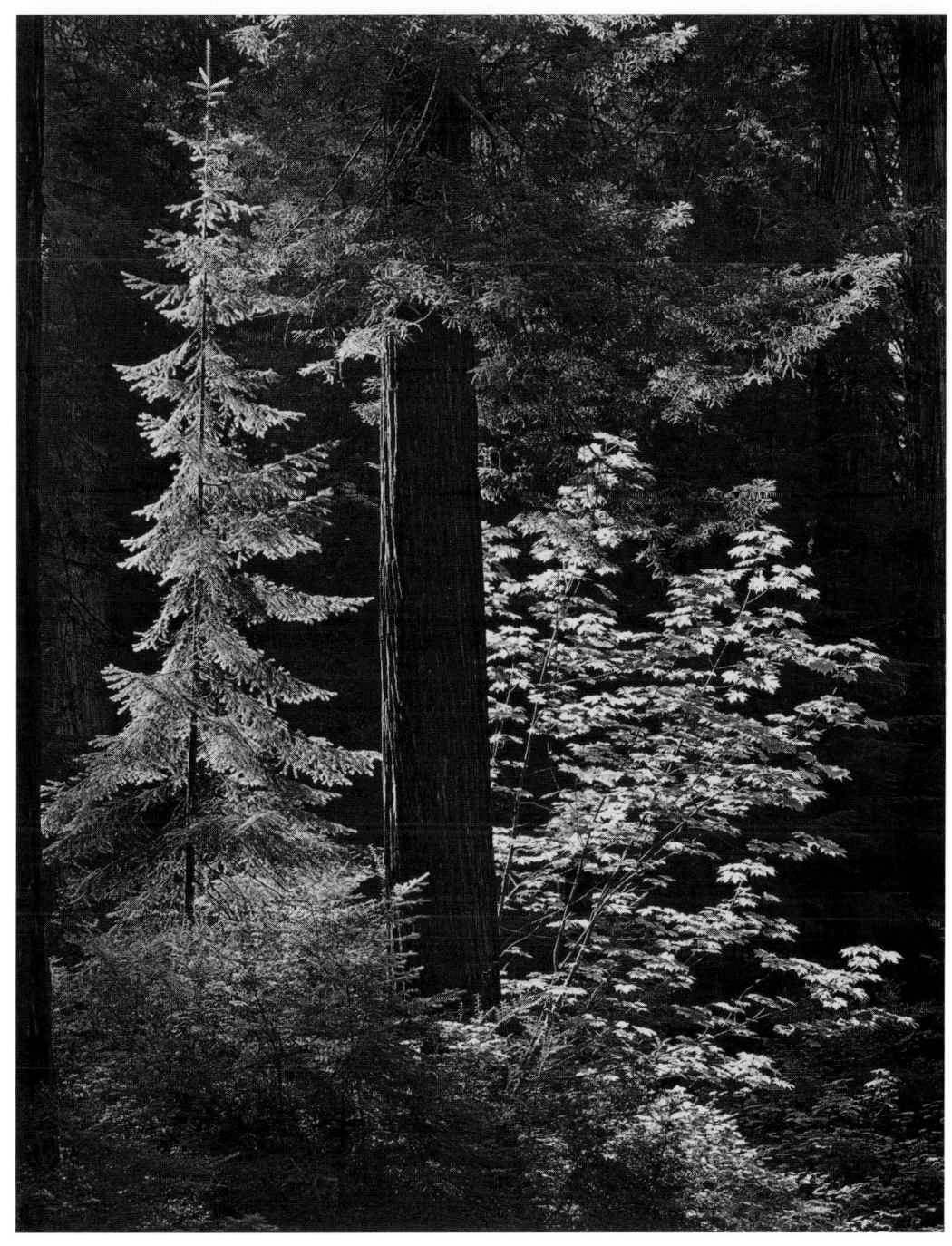

"Prairie Creek, Redwoods, California," 1983

Silver gelatin print, *Portfolio XIII: Photographs in Four Decades*

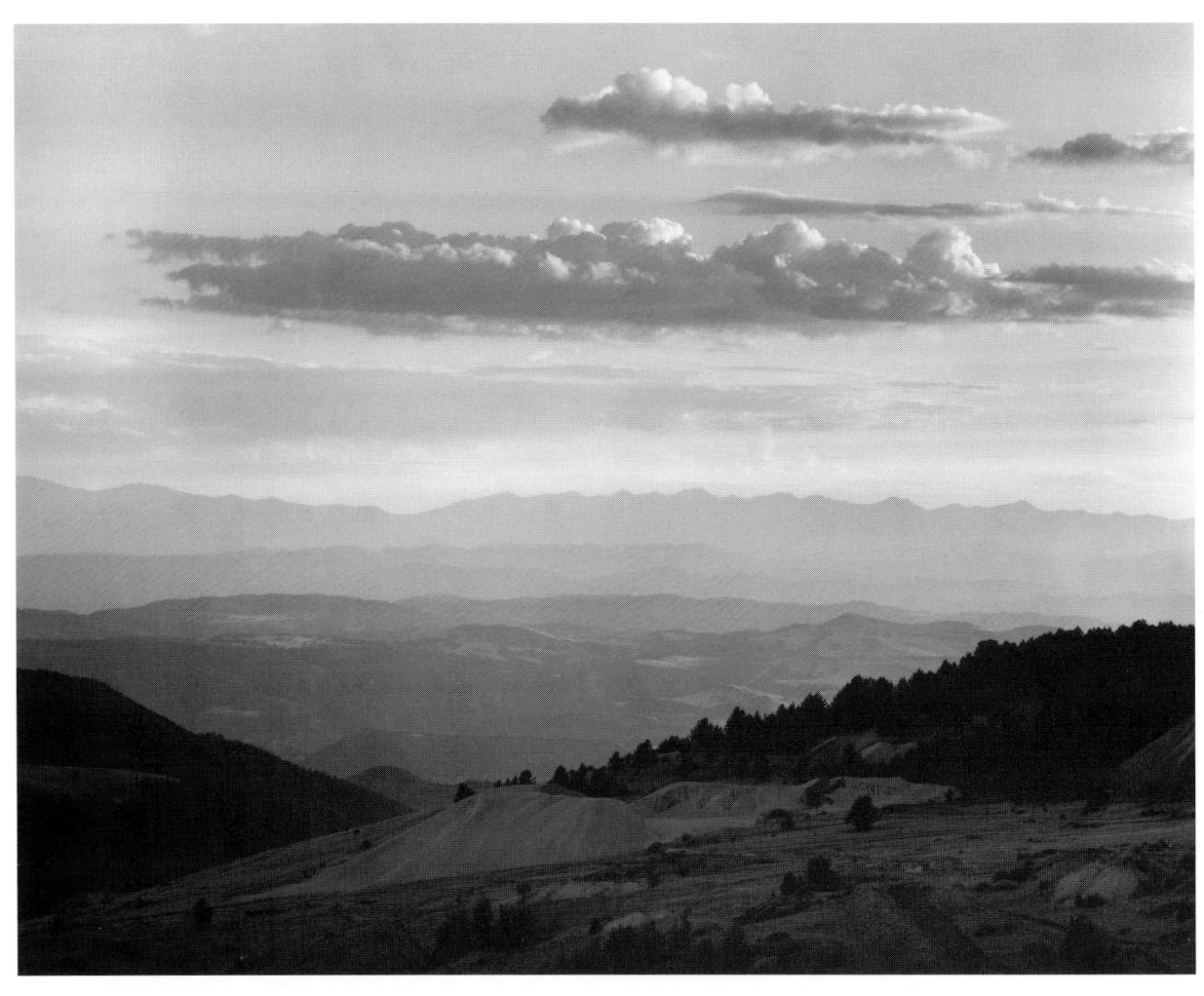

"Sangre de Cristo Range," 1980

Silver gelatin print, *Portfolio III: Victor*

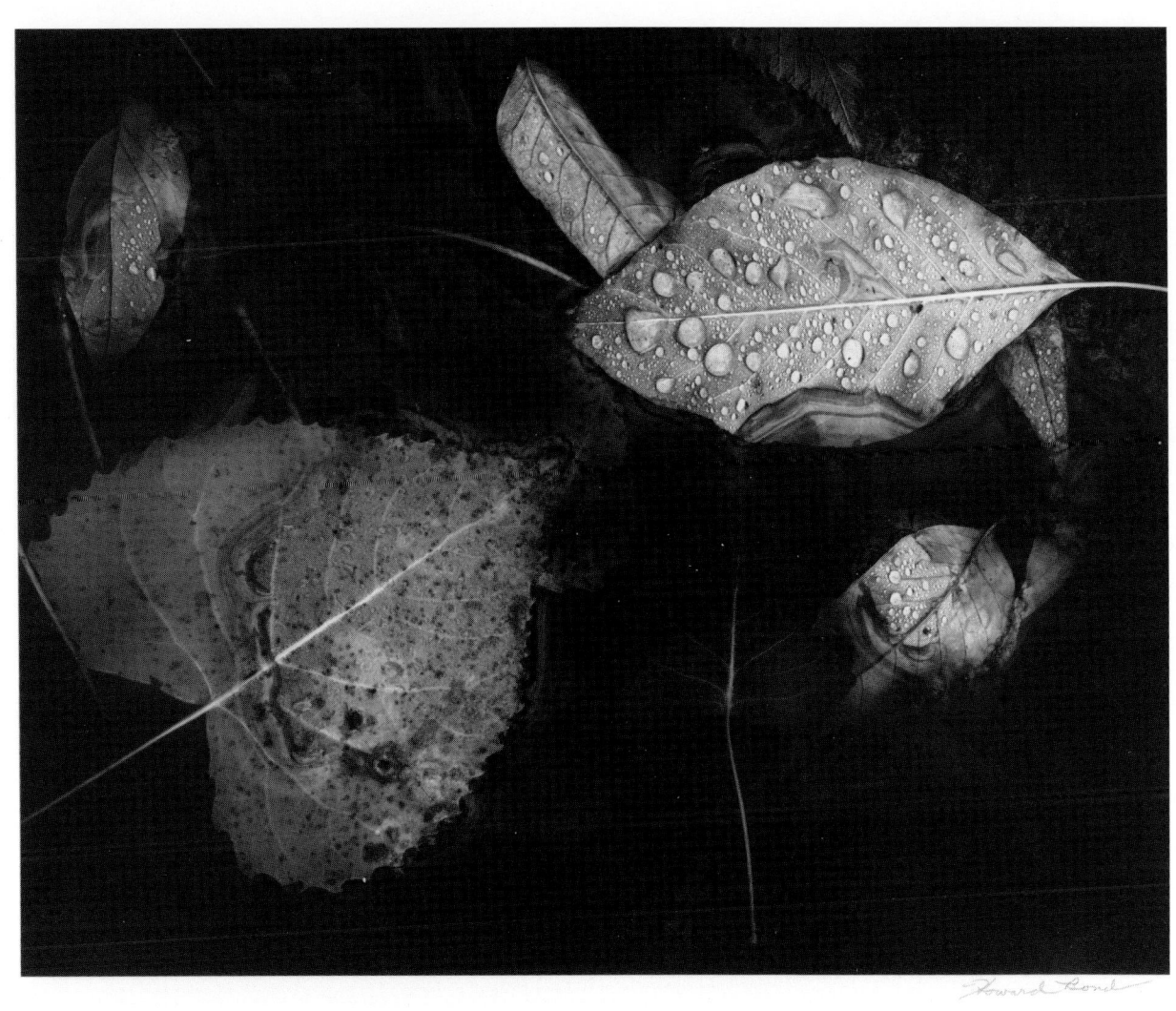

"Leaves with Rain," 1975

Silver gelatin print, *Portfolio IV: Huron River*

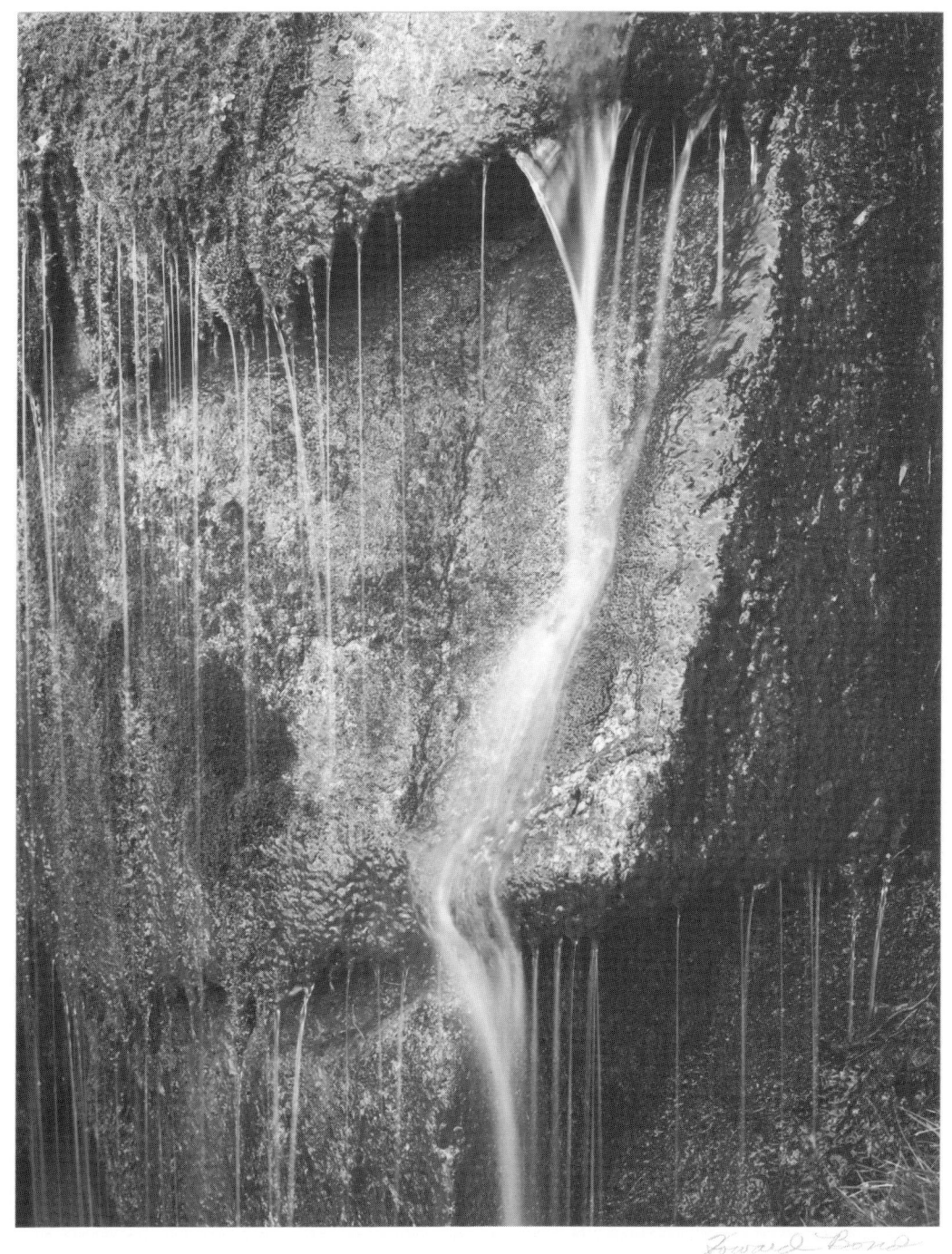

"Rivulet, Chicago Basin," 1982

Silver gelatin print, *Portfolio V: Colorado*

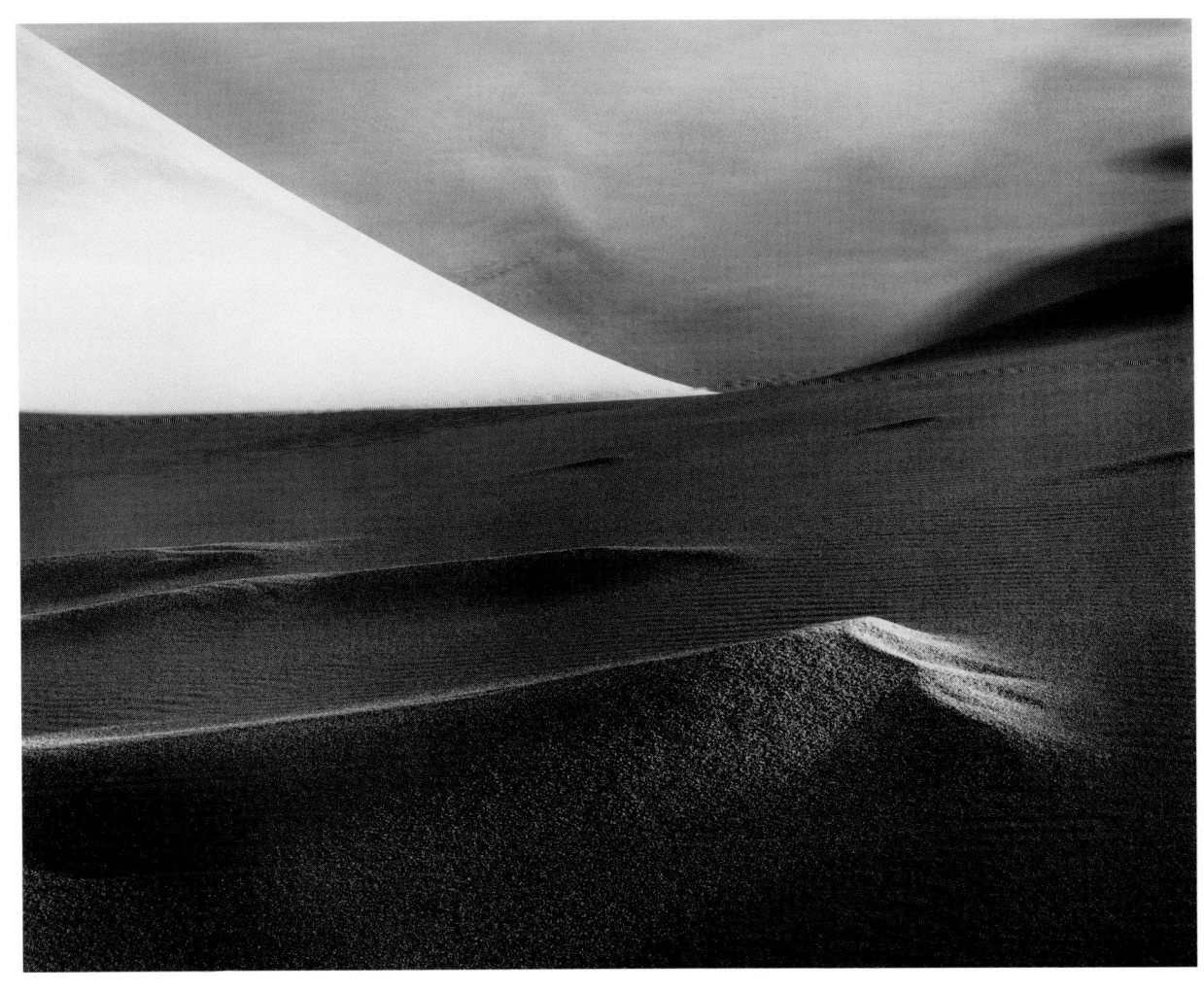

"Light Triangle," 1991

Silver gelatin print, *Portfolio XII: Great Sand Dunes*

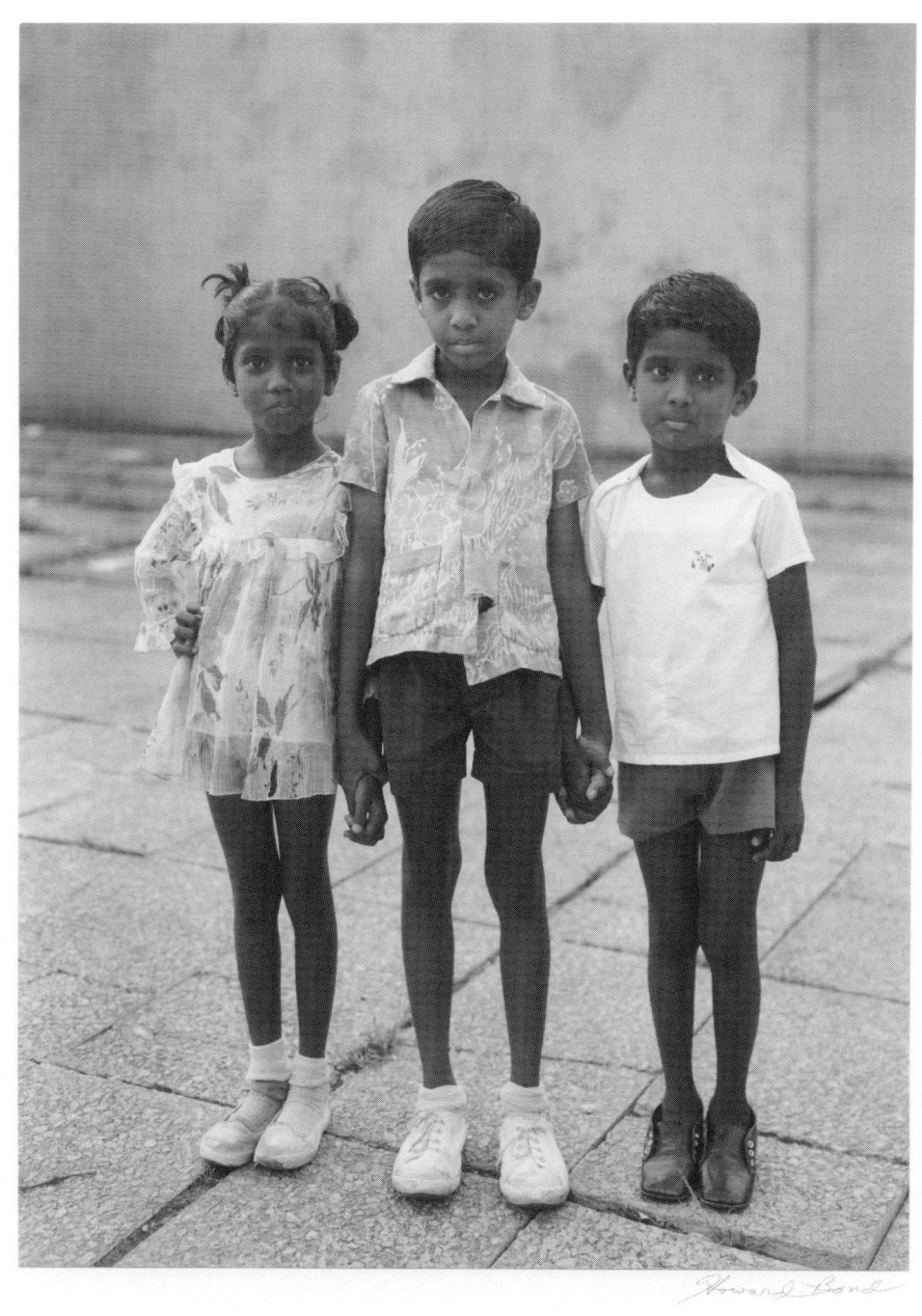

"Brothers and Sister, Kuala Lumpur, Malaysia," 1973

Silver gelatin print, *Portfolio VIII: People and Places*

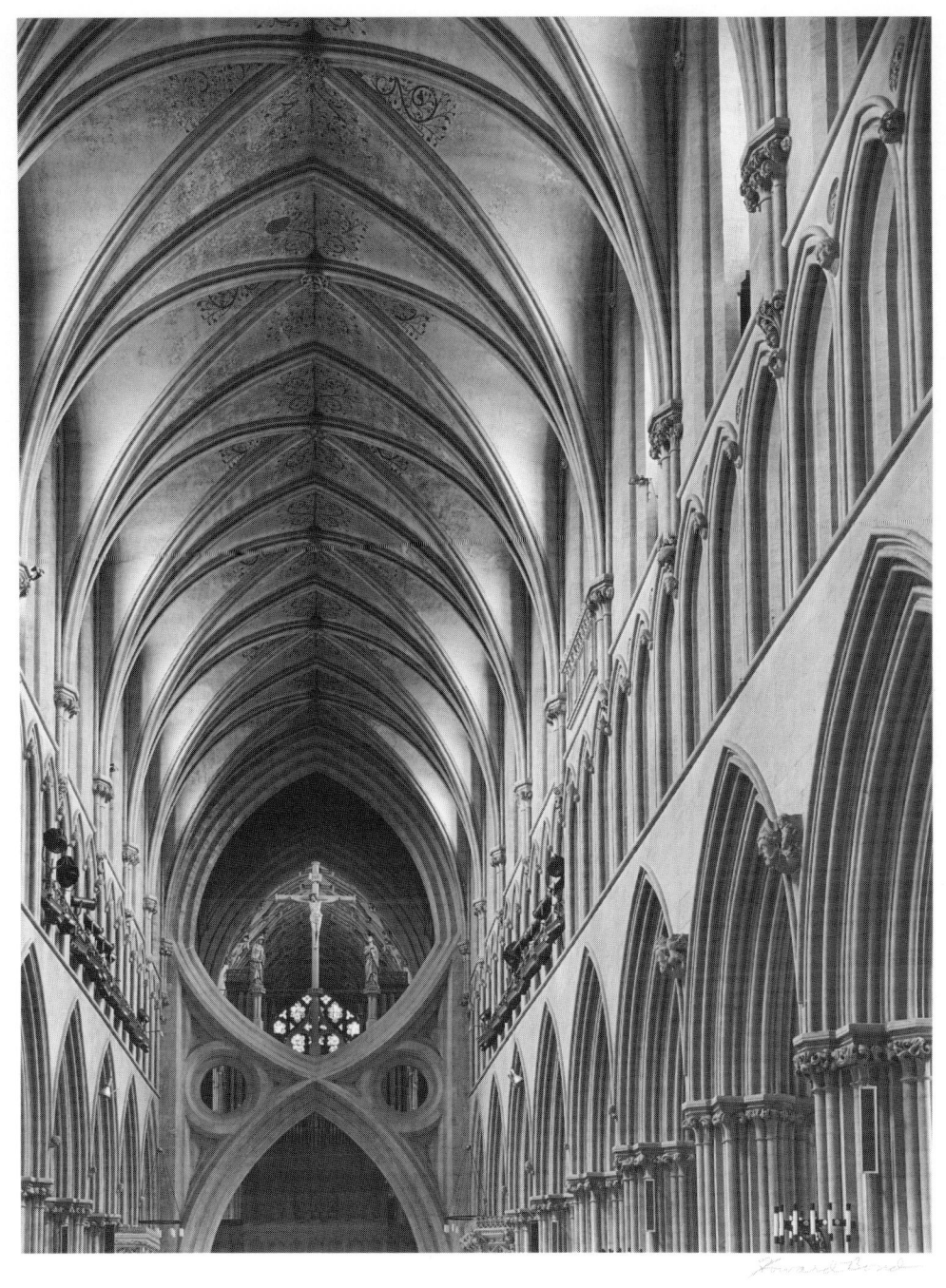

"Nave, Wells," 1982

Silver gelatin print, *Portfolio XIV: English Churches*

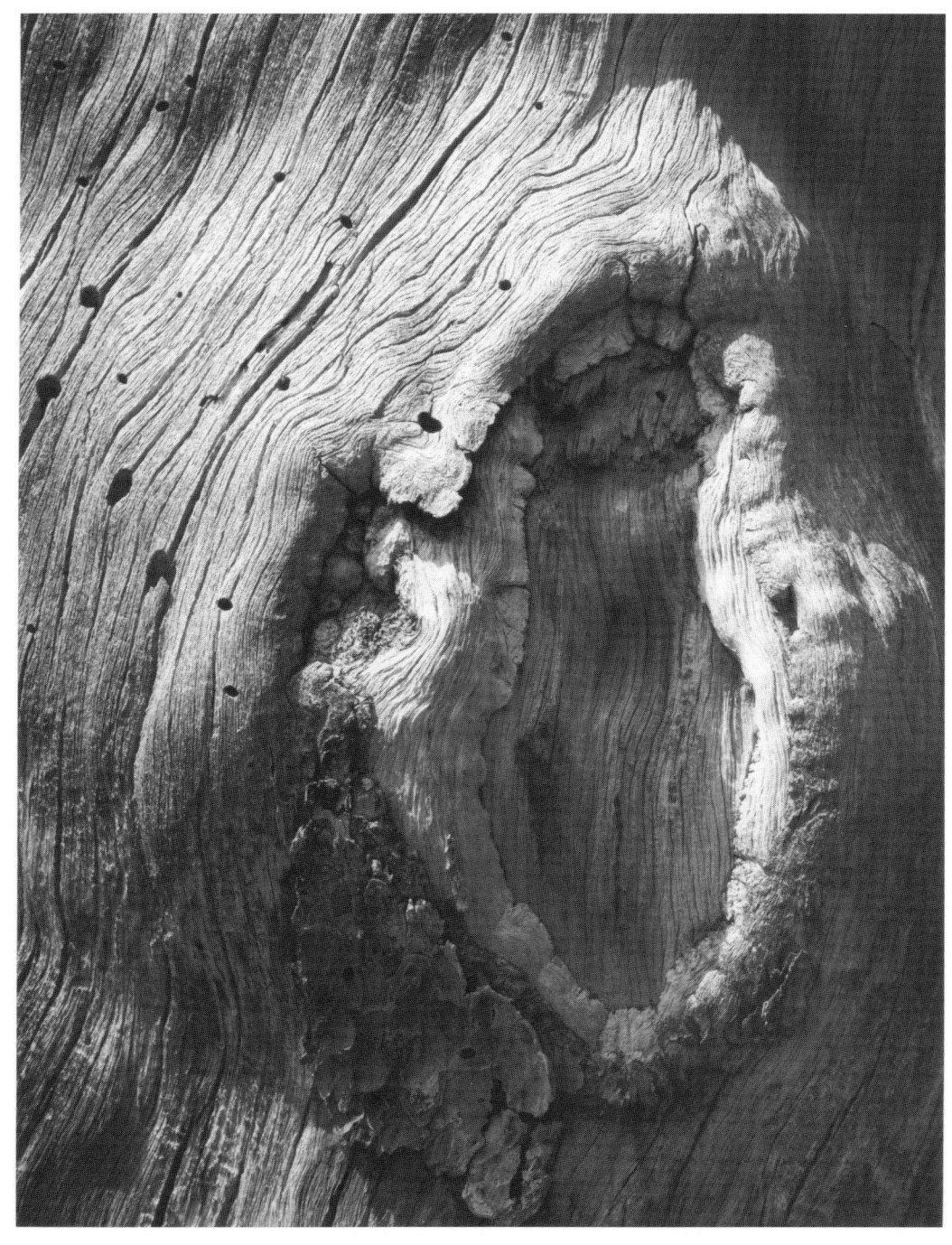

"Dead Tree, White River," 1983

Silver gelatin print, *Portfolio V: Colorado*

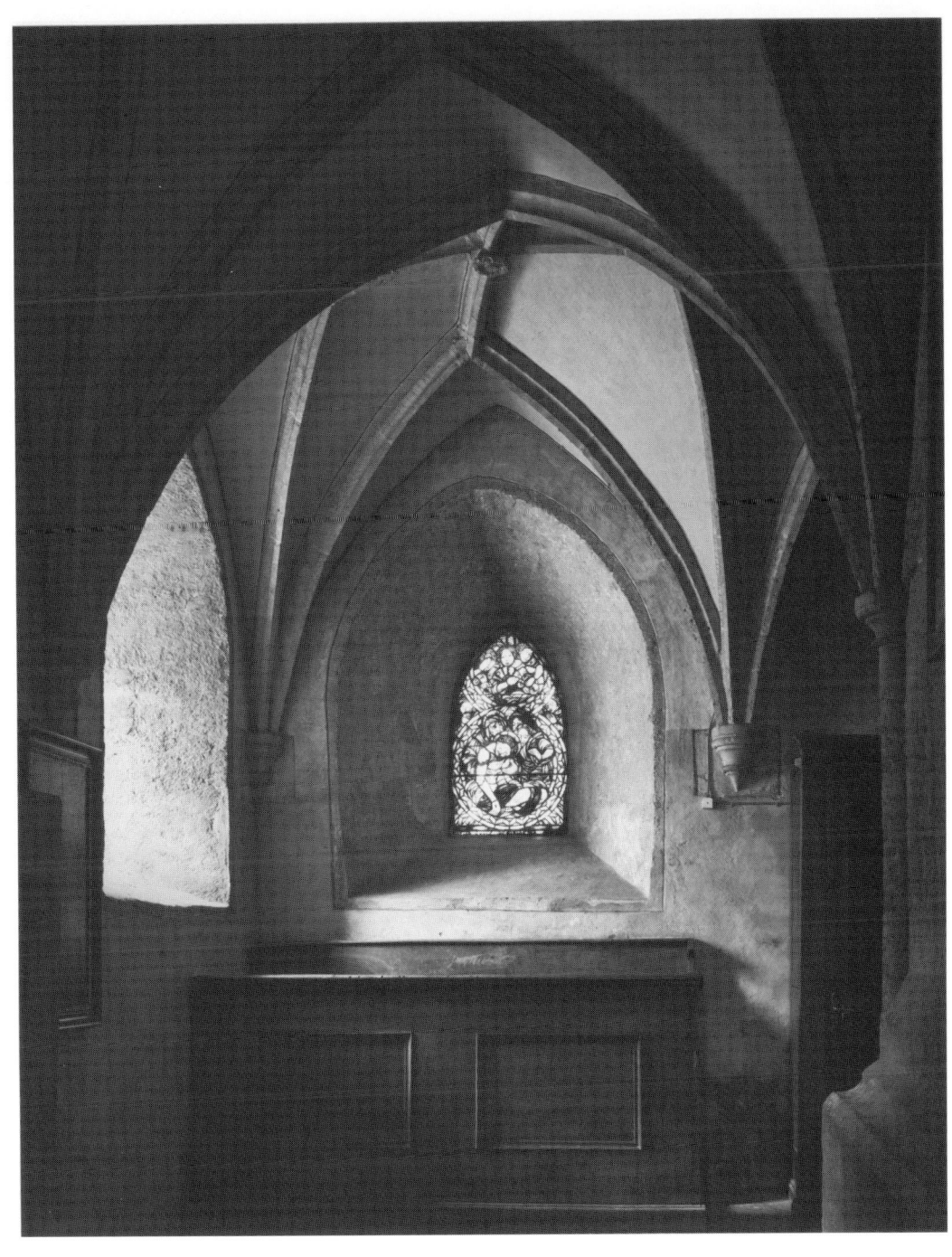

"Church Window, Maria Saal," 1978

Silver gelatin print, *Portfolio II: Austria*

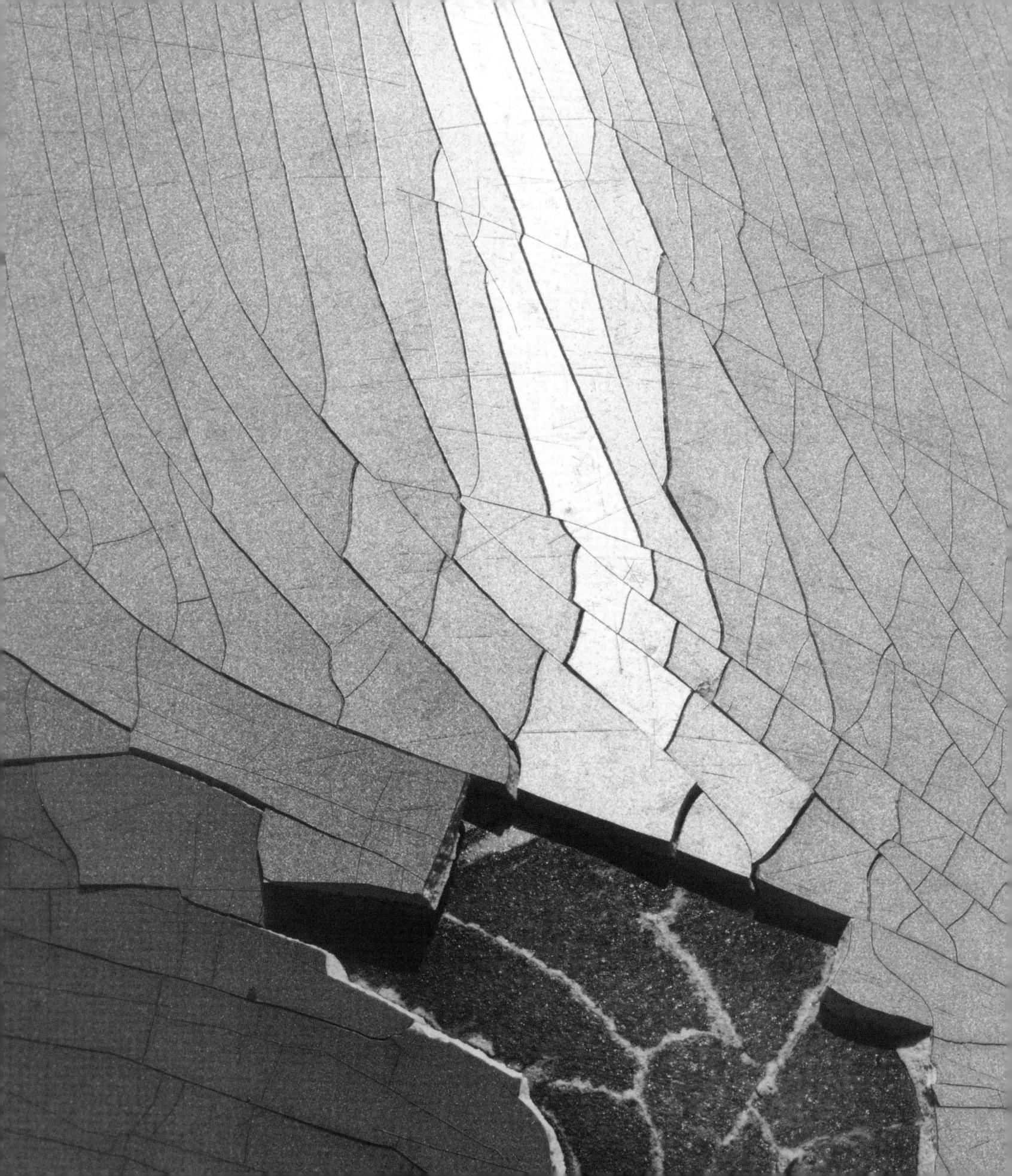

Texture

Large-format photography lends itself to rich texture. Often it is these detailed textures that create the illusion of a three-dimensional space. The photographs here show the pitted, cracked, crystallized, or silky smooth texture of objects. The viewer can contemplate the tonal variations, finding complexity and movement in the surfaces of objects. In many of these images it is absence that provides complexity; the spaces of dark air or frozen water allow other textures to emerge more boldly. In "Ice Opening, Huron River, Michigan" (1977), ice and snow cling to a fallen tree while, just behind, exposed water gently laps against the almost fully frozen surface.

In other photographs the detailed textures play against each other. The face of an old woman contrasts with the weave of her dress and the curtain hanging in her window. Another image combines the textures of foam, rocks, and a sandy beach.

Bond uses framing and composition skillfully, defining areas of complex pattern and texture so intense that the viewer never thinks of what lies outside the frame.

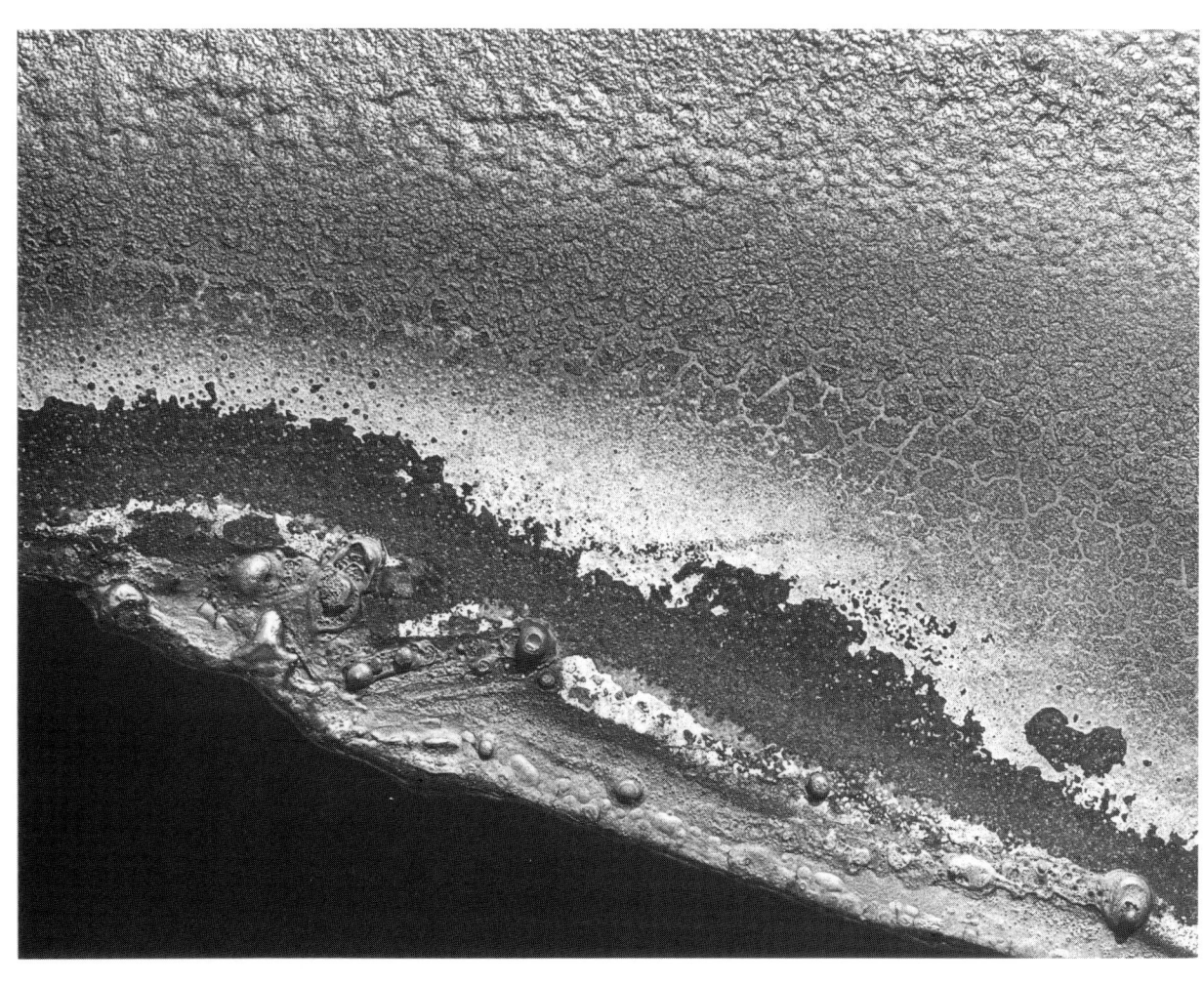

"Nixon Auto Parts No. 20," 1986

Silver gelatin print, *Portfolio XX: Abstraction*

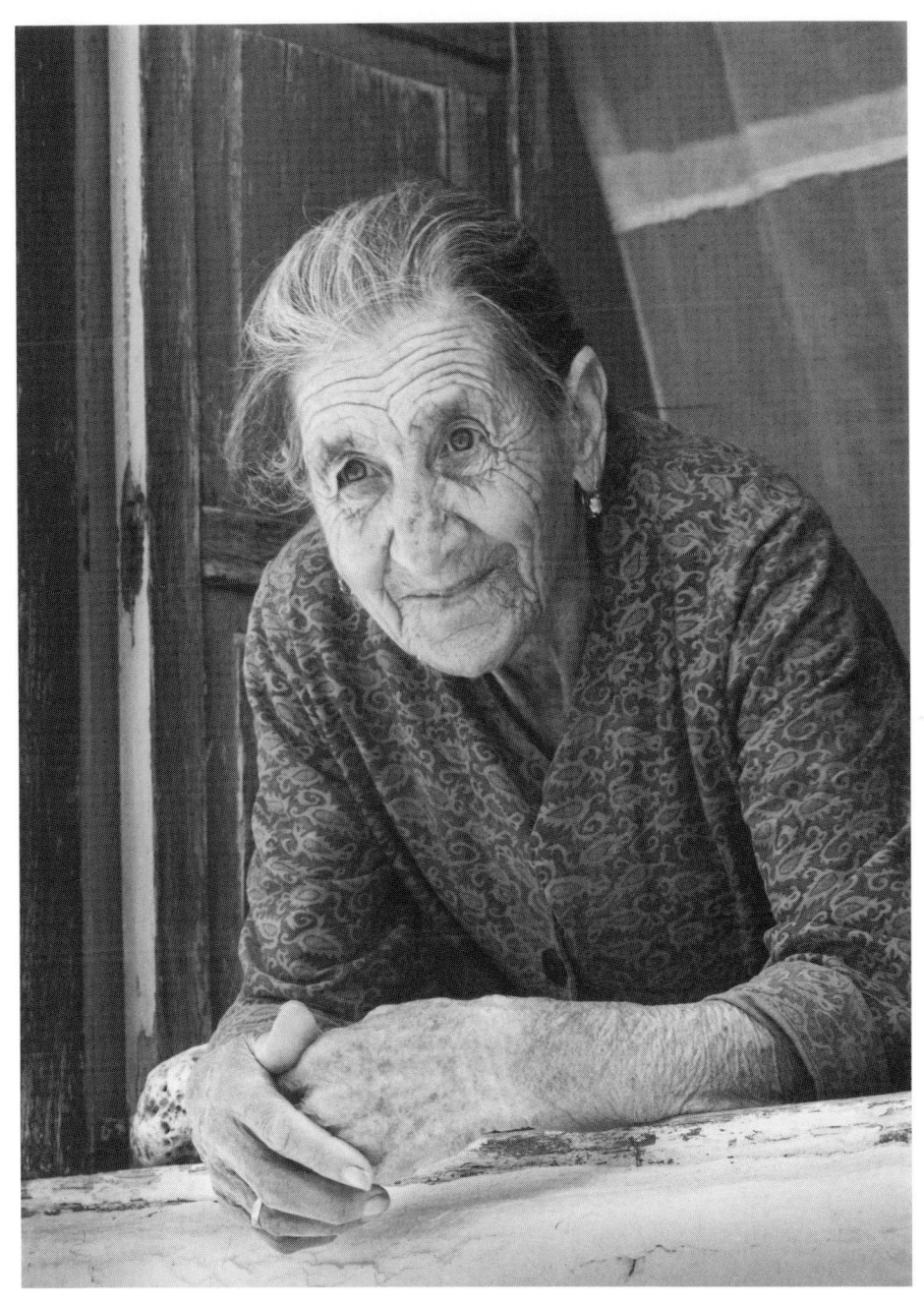

"Woman in Window, Naoussa, Paros, Greece," 1985

Silver gelatin print, *Portfolio VI: Greek Islands*

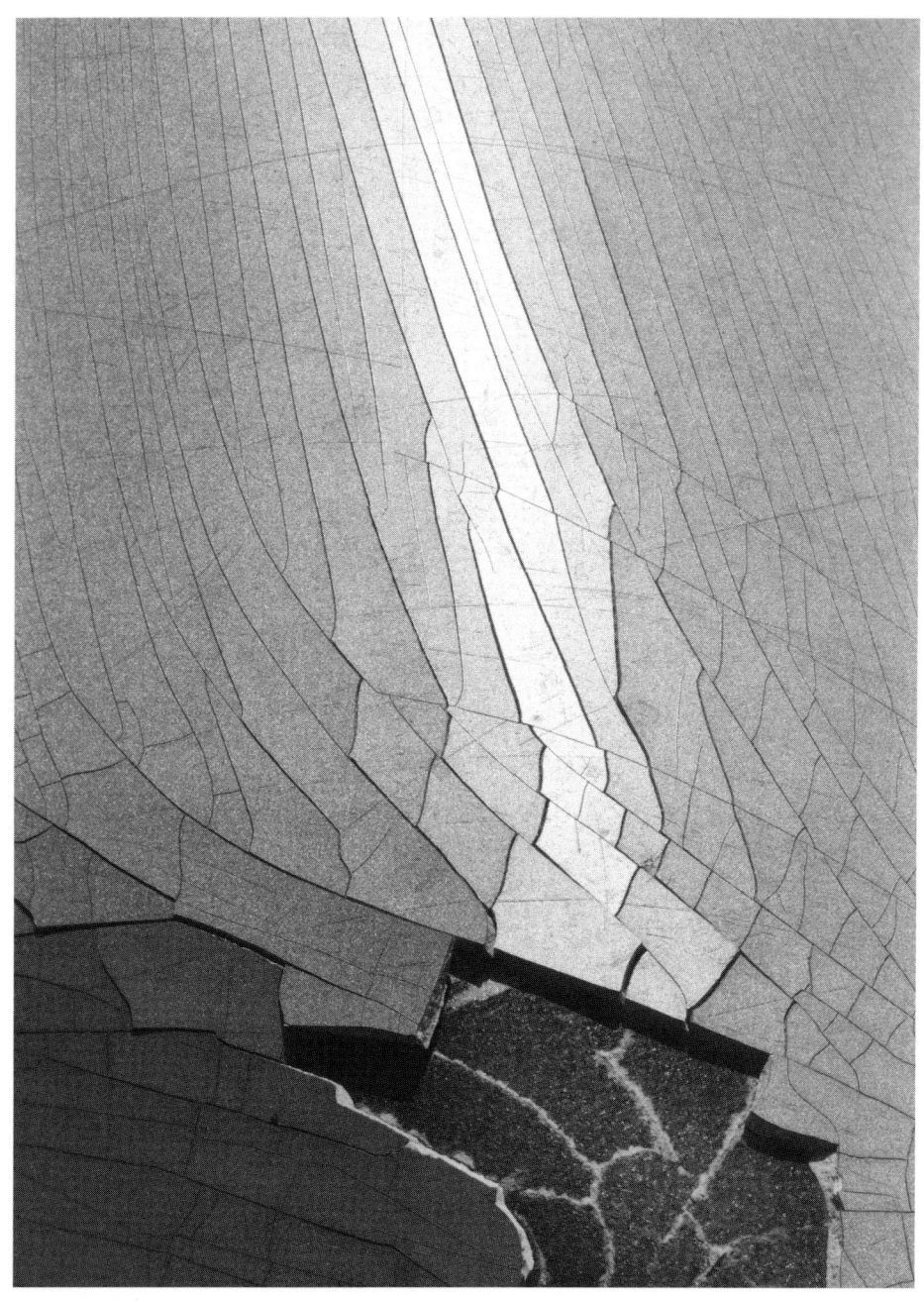

"Nixon Auto Parts No. 1, Michigan," 1986

Silver gelatin print, *Portfolio VII: Proximity*

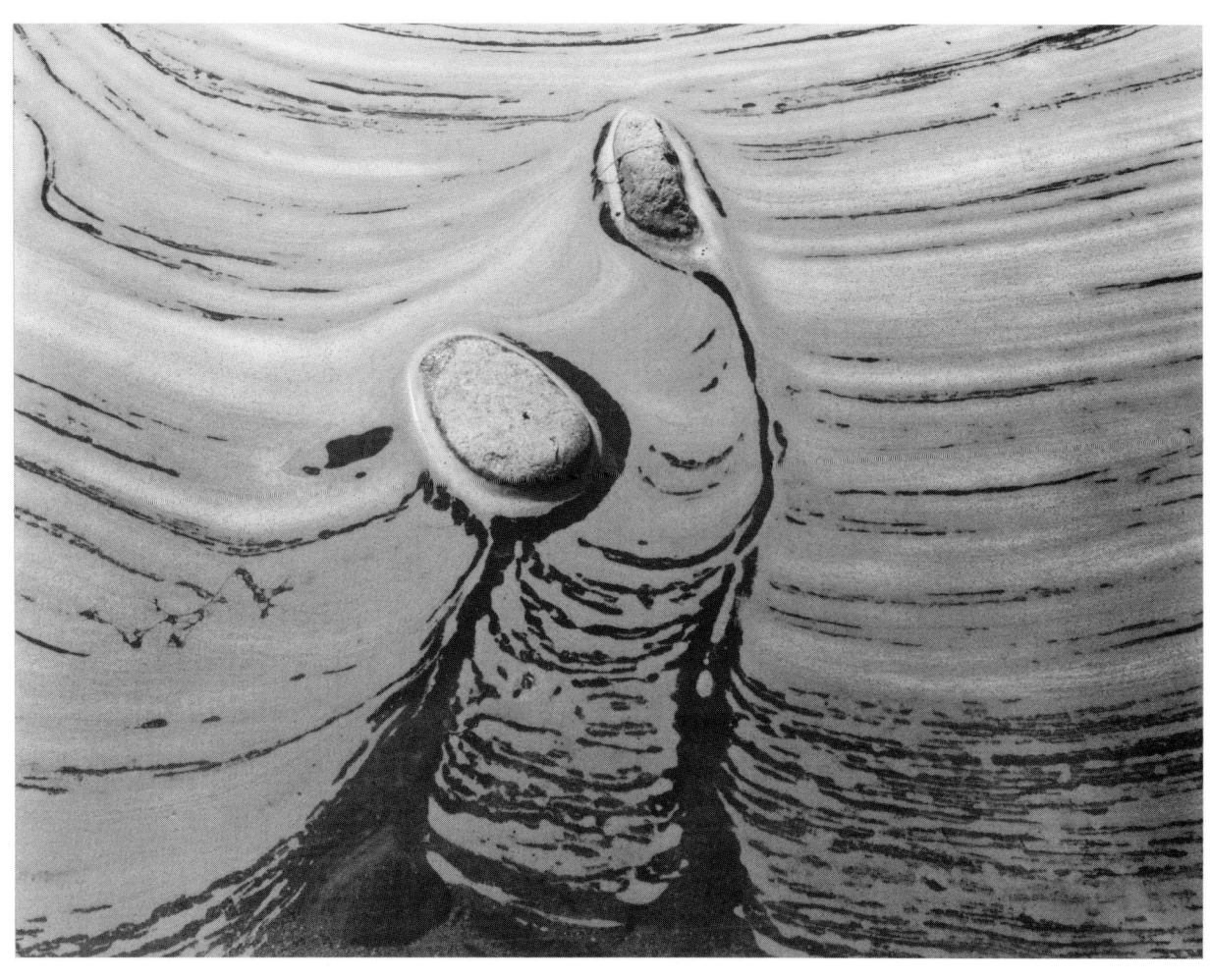

"Rocks and Foam, Sand River," 1979

Silver gelatin print, *Portfolio IX: Ontario*

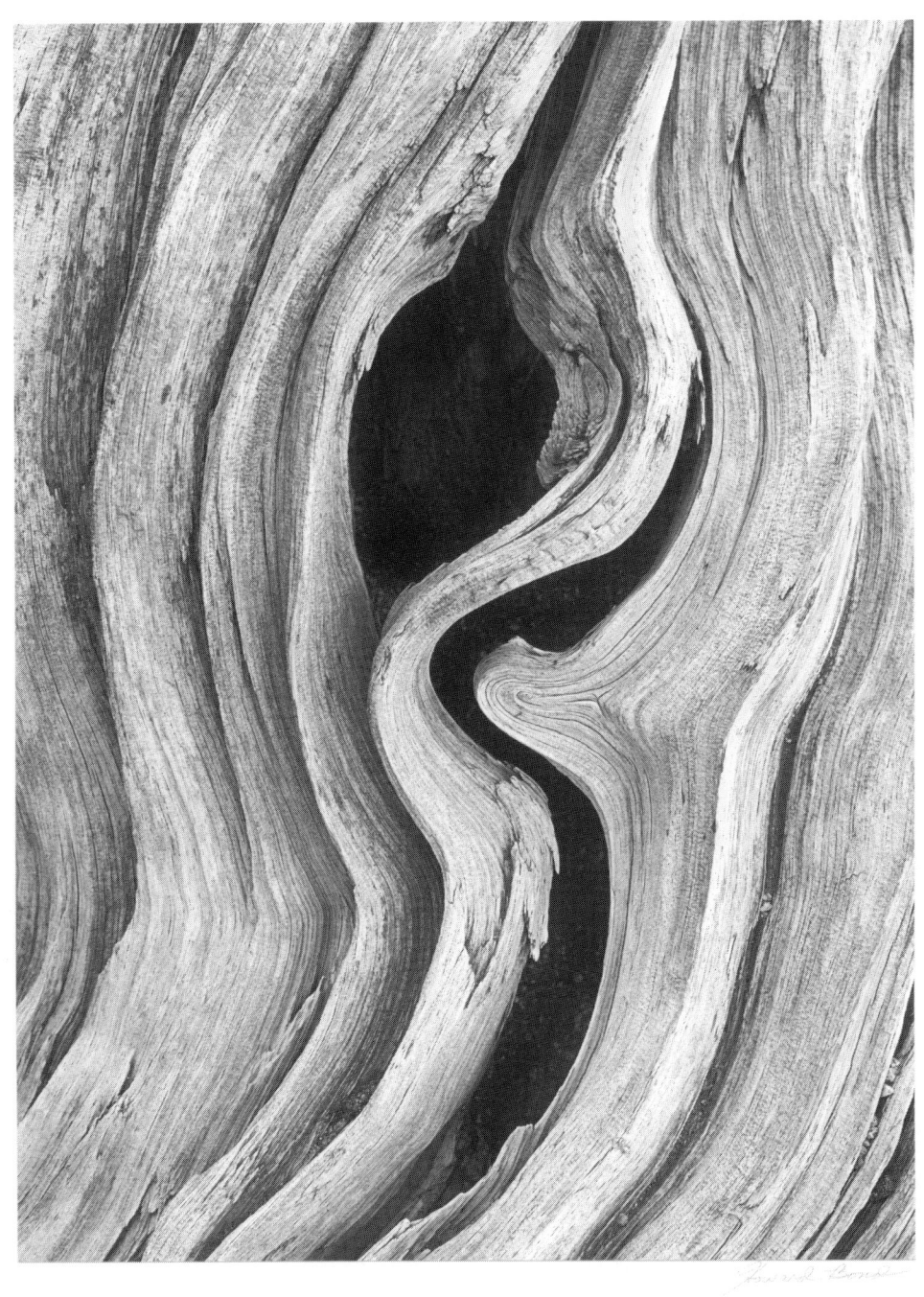

"Bristlecone Pine No. 2, Colorado," 1993

Silver gelatin print, *Portfolio XV: Bristlecone Pines*

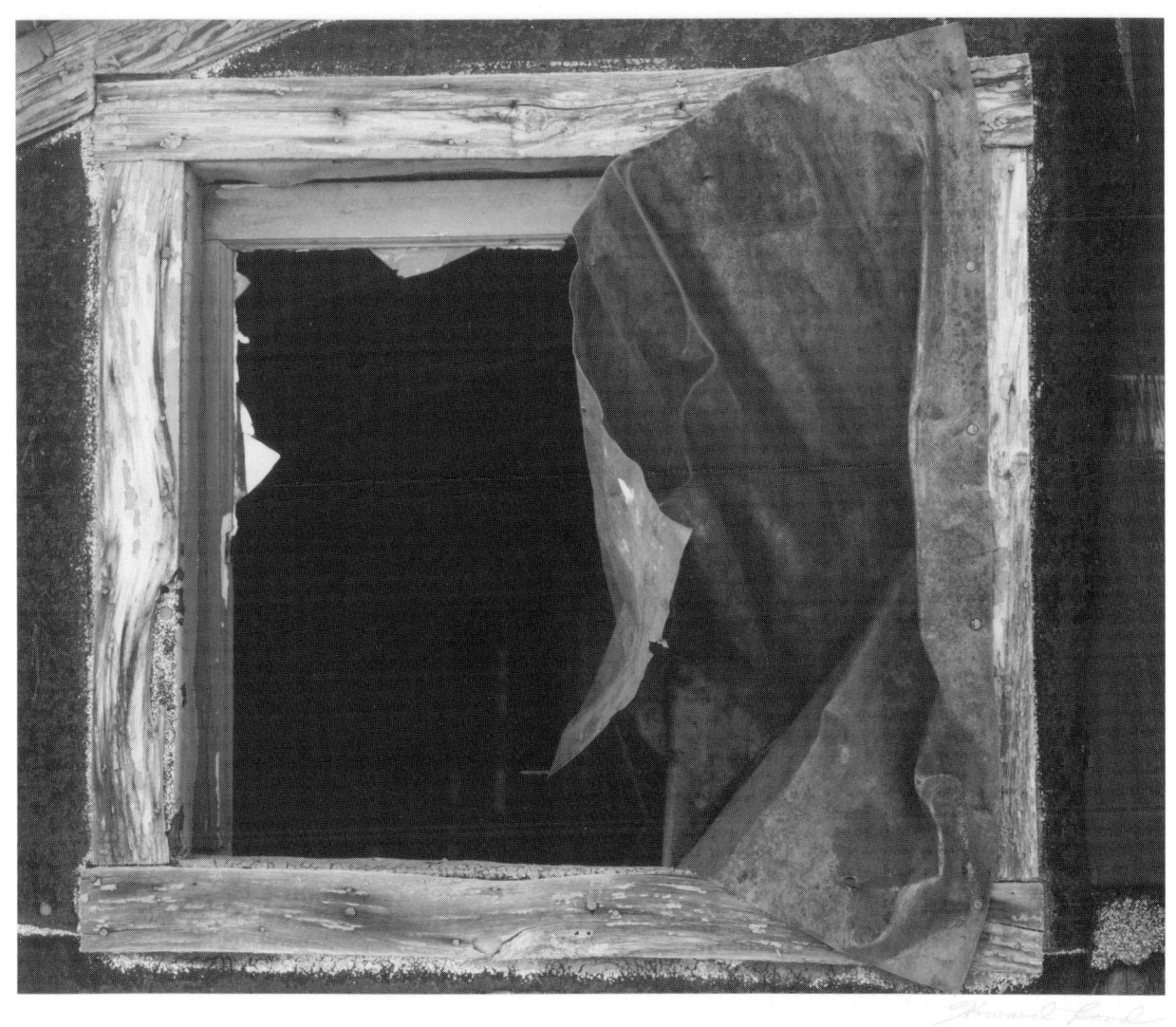

"Window," 1980

Silver gelatin print, *Portfolio III: Victor*

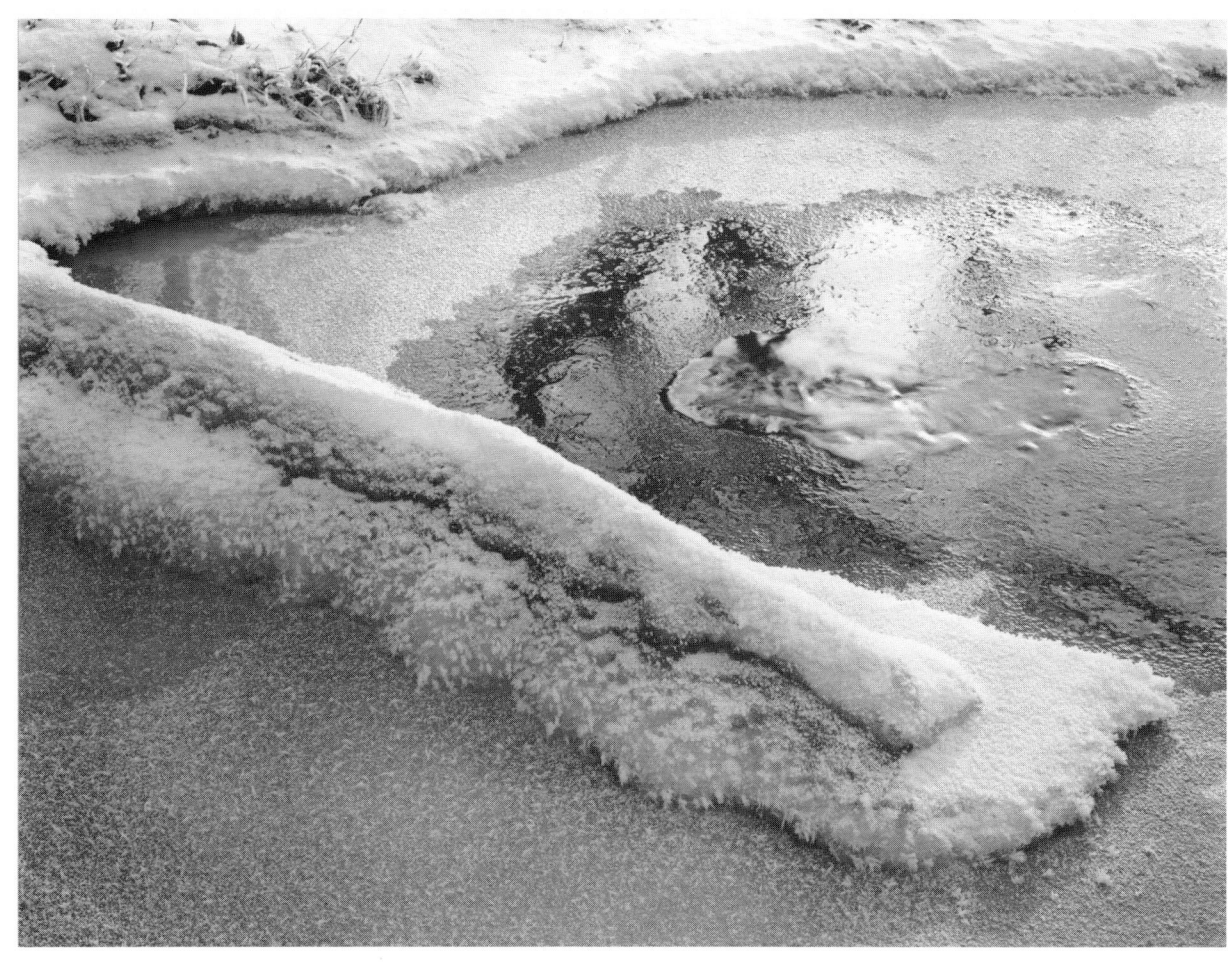

"Ice Opening, Huron River, Michigan," 1977

Silver gelatin print, *Portfolio X: Contact Prints*

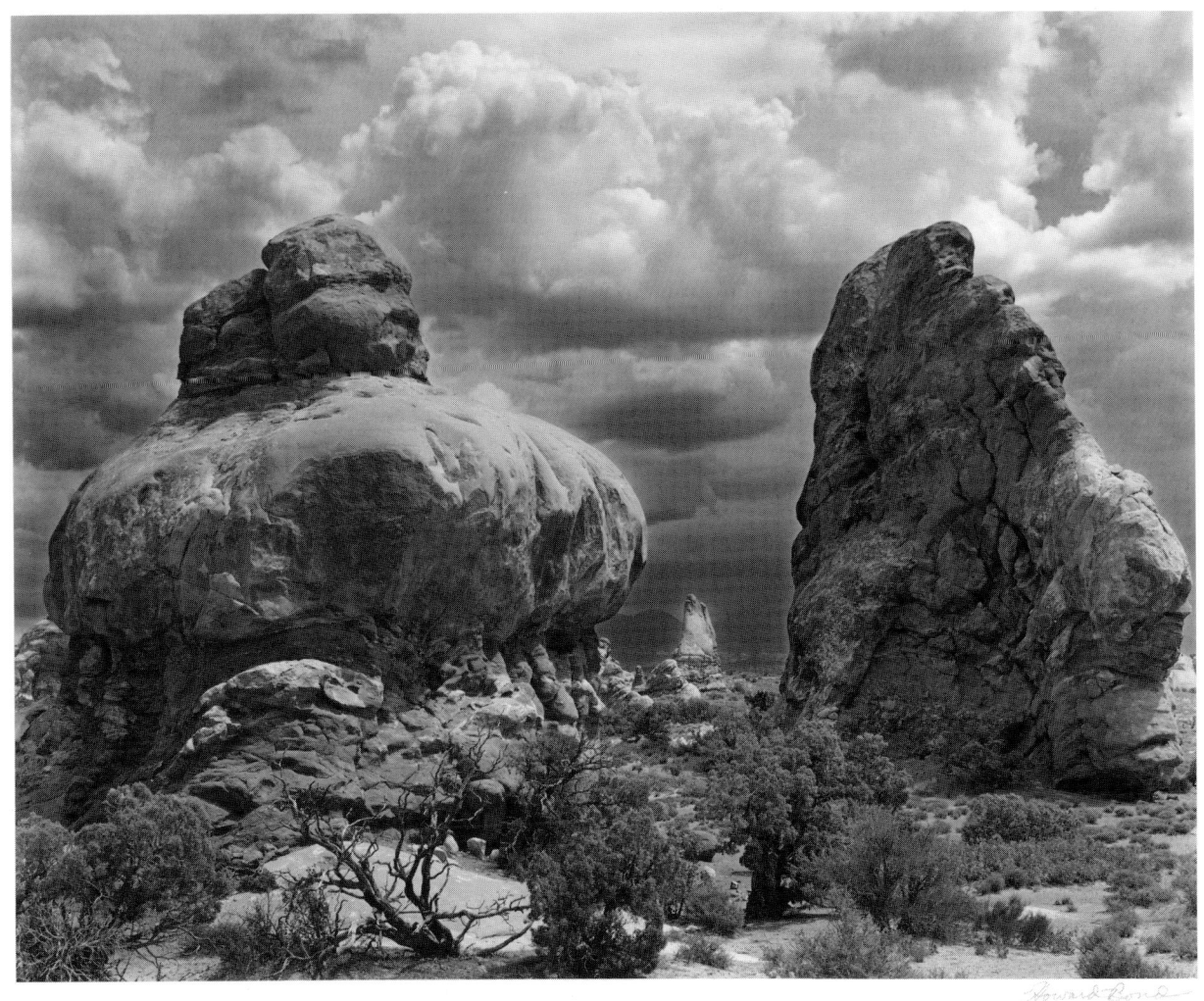

"Monoliths, Arches," 1980

Silver gelatin print, *Portfolio XIX: Sandstone Country*

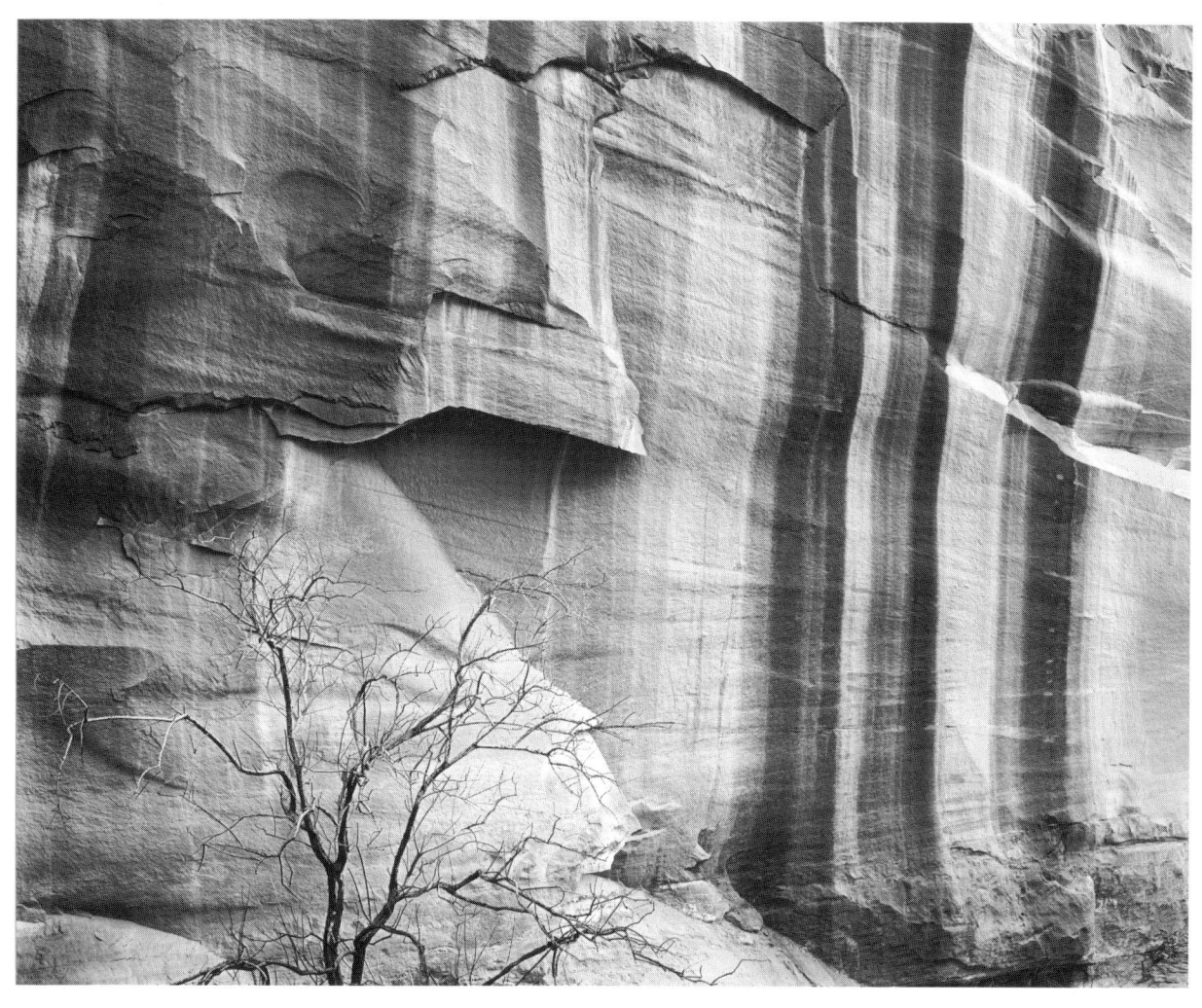

"Desert Varnish, Utah," 2002

Silver gelatin print, *Portfolio XIX: Sandstone Country*

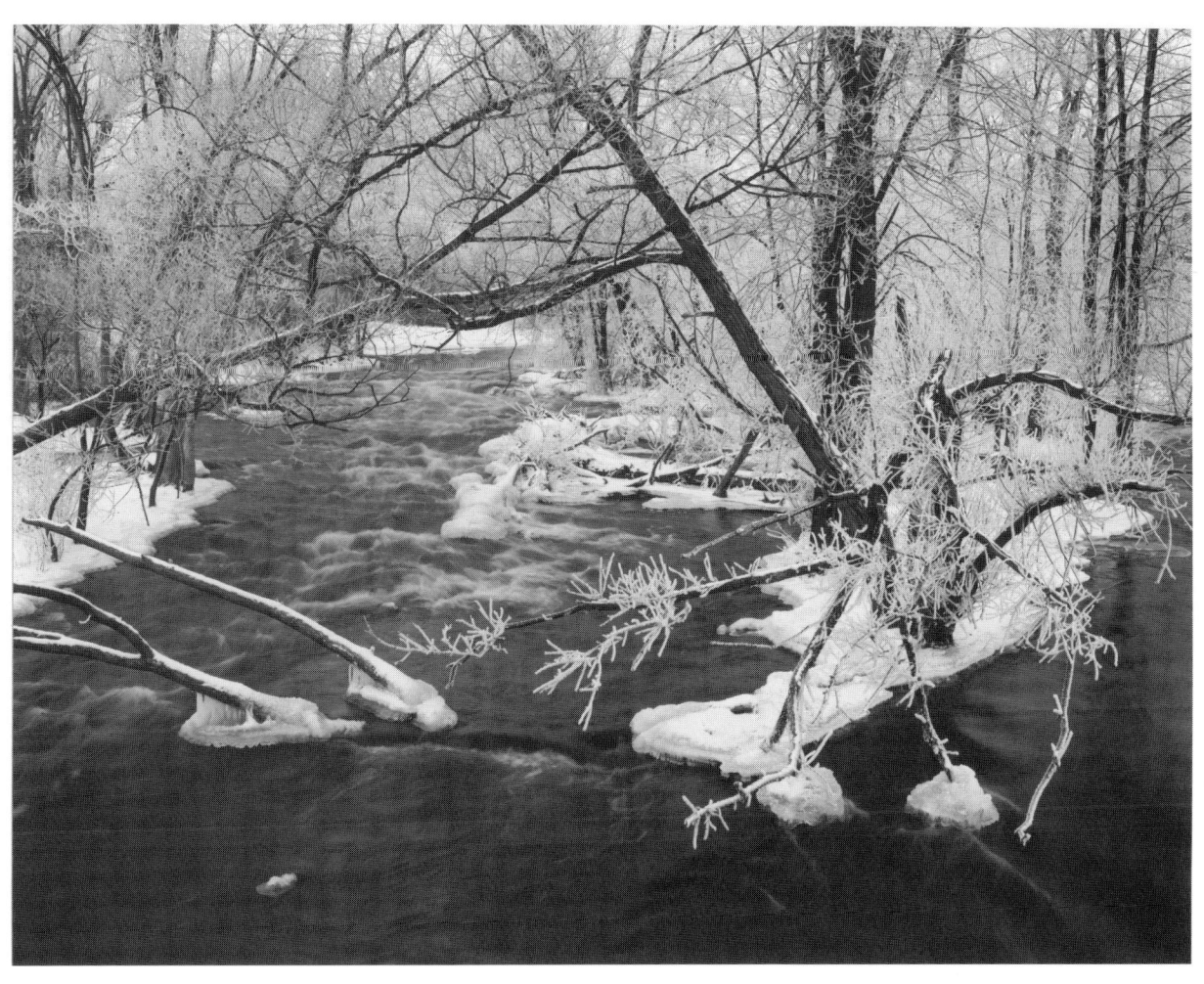

"Delhi Rapid, Winter," 1974

Silver gelatin print, *Portfolio IV: Huron River*

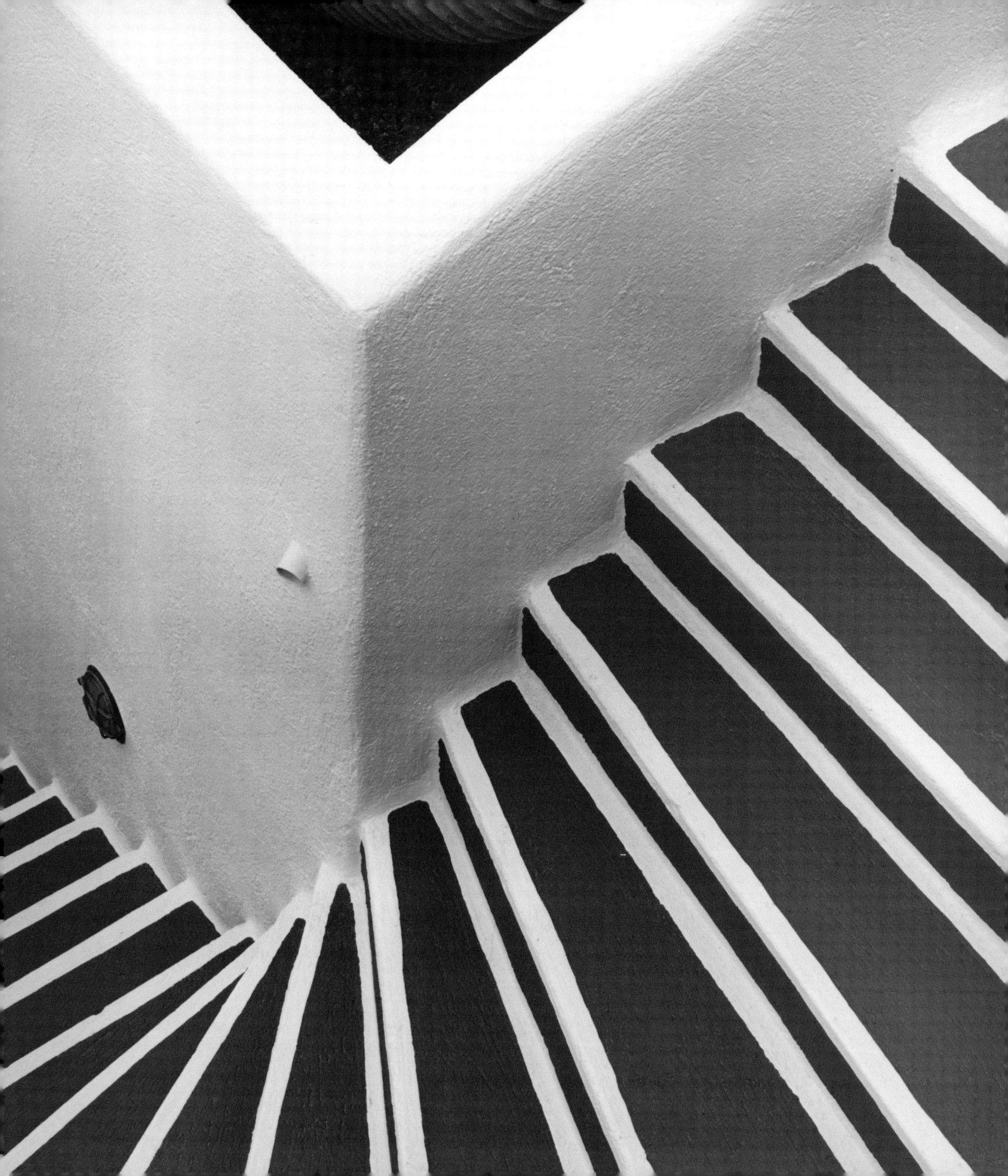

Pattern

Each pattern is unique like a fingerprint or a snowflake. Images in this selection demonstrate Bond's ability to see patterns that others tend to overlook. These photographs, composed with a controlled use of line and shape, display the strong graphic quality that is a dominant feature of Howard Bond's work. He juxtaposes shapes and tones to create images full of rhythm and harmony.

In "Ceiling Support, Gloucester" (2000), Bond created a symmetrical composition out of a church structure, defining and displaying its repeating embellishments like musical notes on a page. In contrast, his "Window, Woebley" (1982) shows the asymmetry between the church window and the cascading shadow it casts on the wall.

In "Sandstone Pattern, Arizona" (2001), the sandstone cliffs mimic the sheer curtains of "Curtain, Weathersfield, Michigan" (1983). Both photographs contain strong static lines that are defined by light. The void left by a broken windshield in "Truck Windshield, Michigan" (1980) makes the skyline of mountains almost an inverted vision of "Wall and Ridges" (1991), where sand dunes recede into the distance, swallowing the horizon.

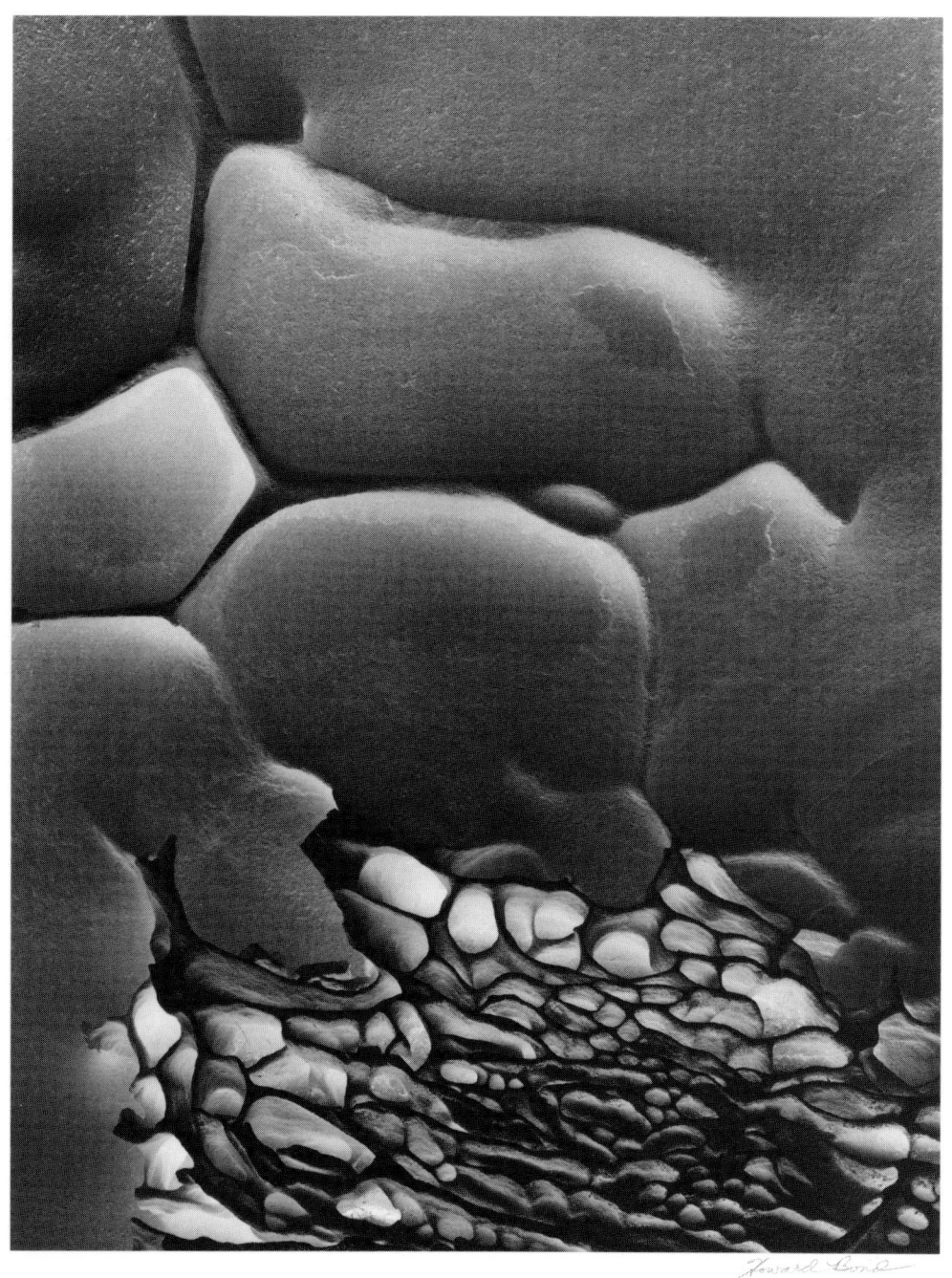

"Honeycomb Rock, Glenburn," 2000

Silver gelatin print, *Portfolio XVII: New Zealand*

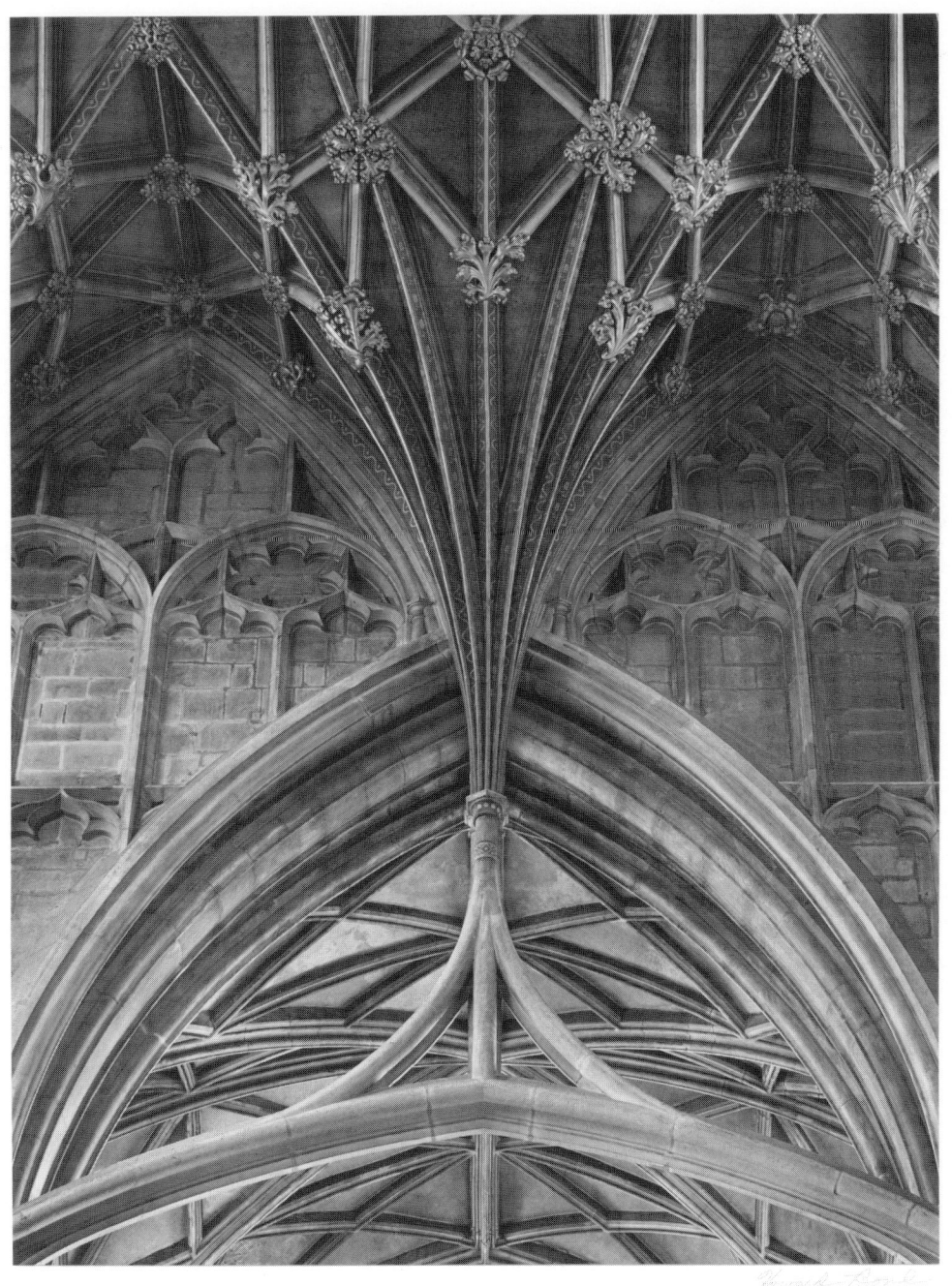

"Ceiling Support, Gloucester," 2000

Silver gelatin print, *Portfolio XVIII: Ten Cathedrals*

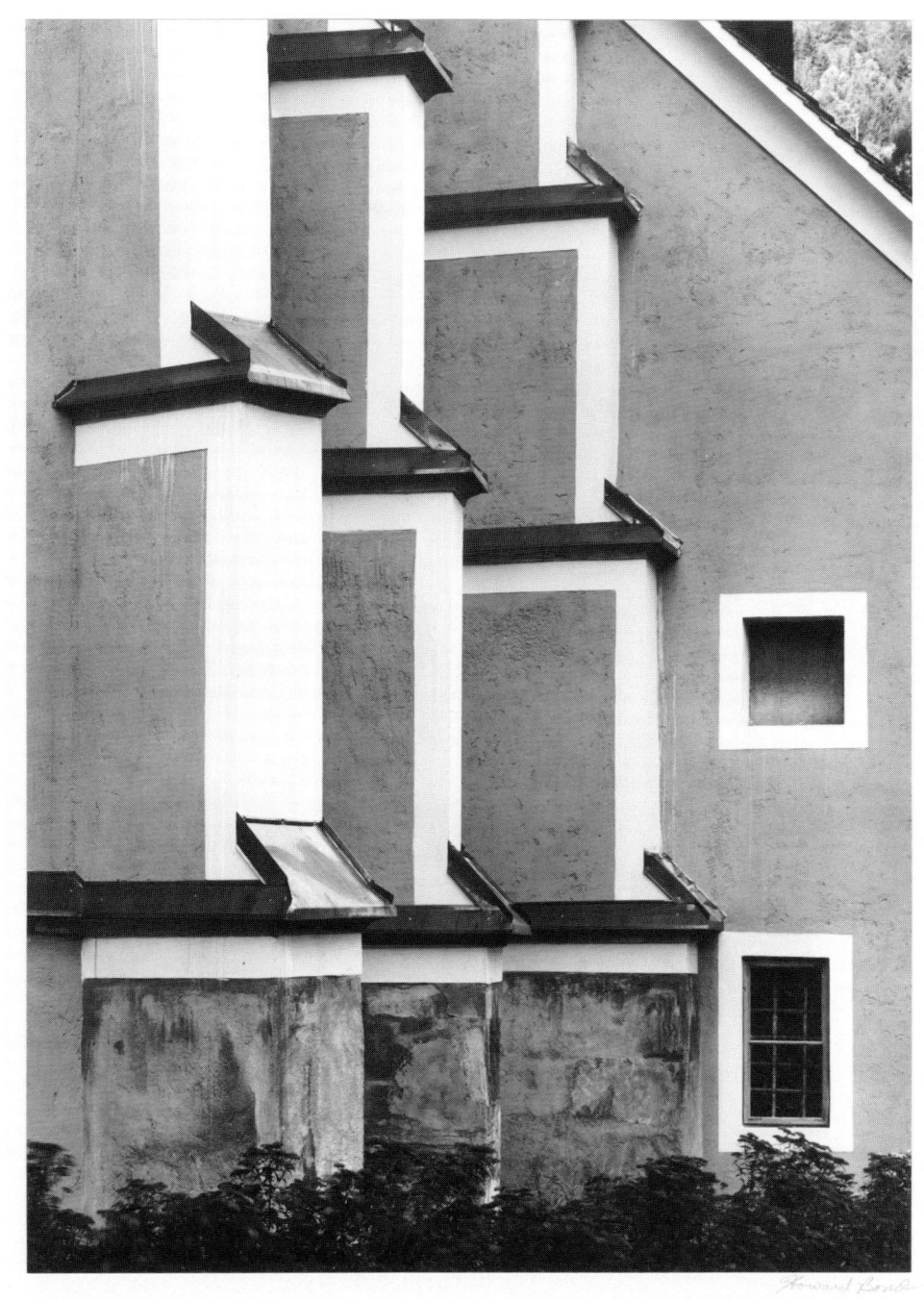

"Church, Friesach," 1978

Silver gelatin print, *Portfolio II: Austria*

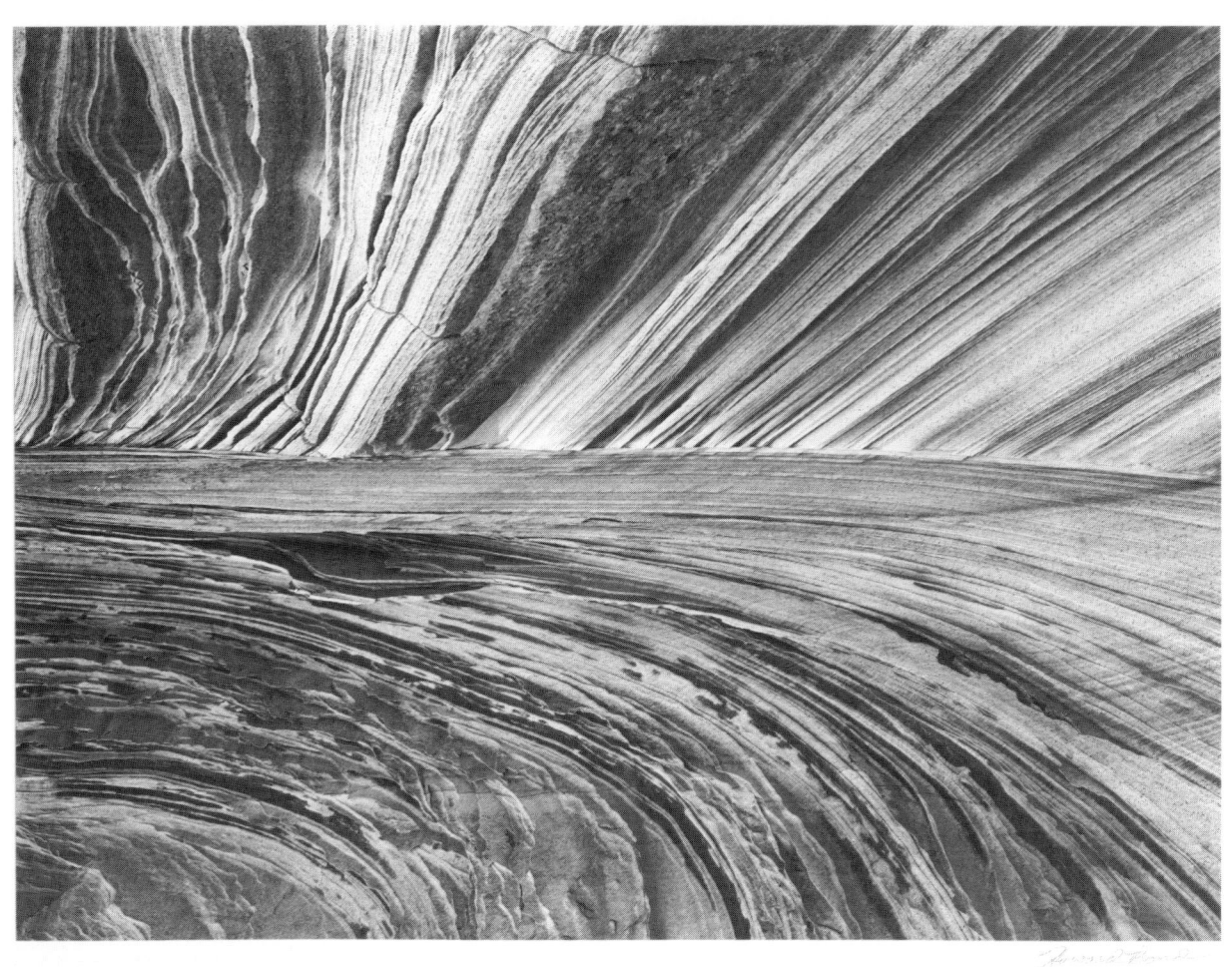

"Sandstone Pattern, Arizona," 2001

Silver gelatin print, *Portfolio XIX: Sandstone Counrty*

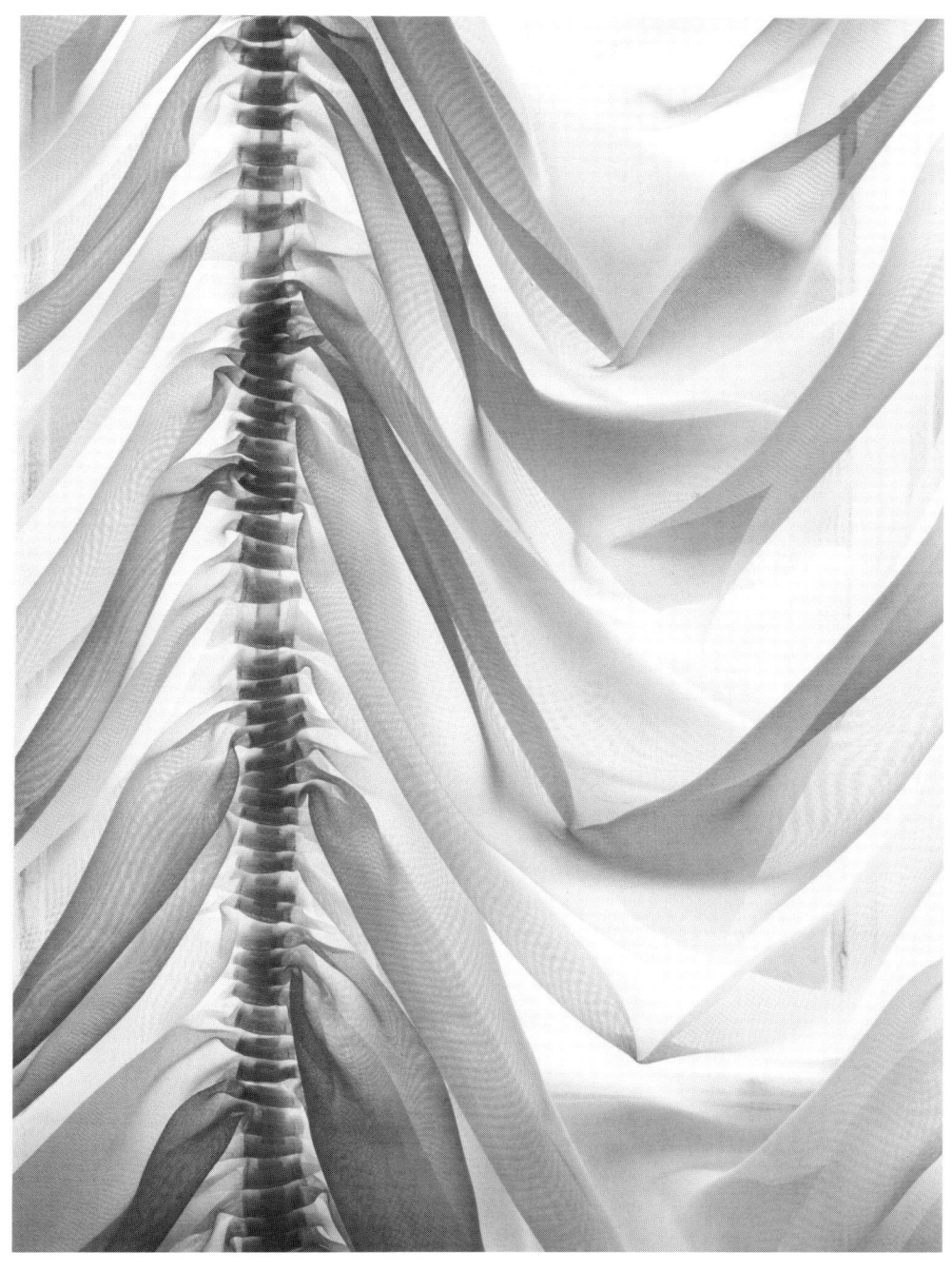

"Curtain, Weathersfield, Michigan," 1983

Silver gelatin print, *Portfolio VII: Proximity*

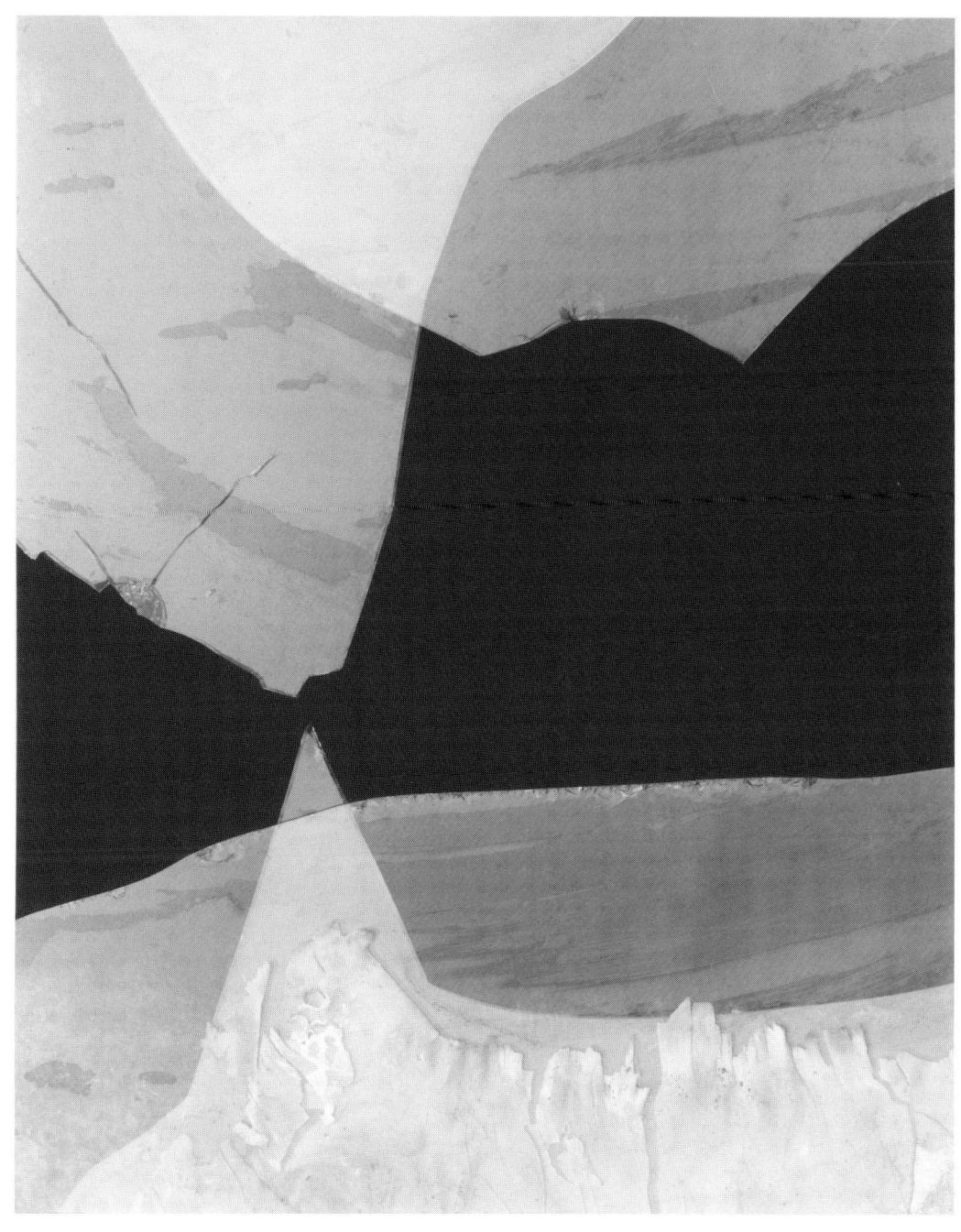

"Truck Windsheid, Michigan," 1980

Silver gelatin print, *Portfolio VII: Proximity*

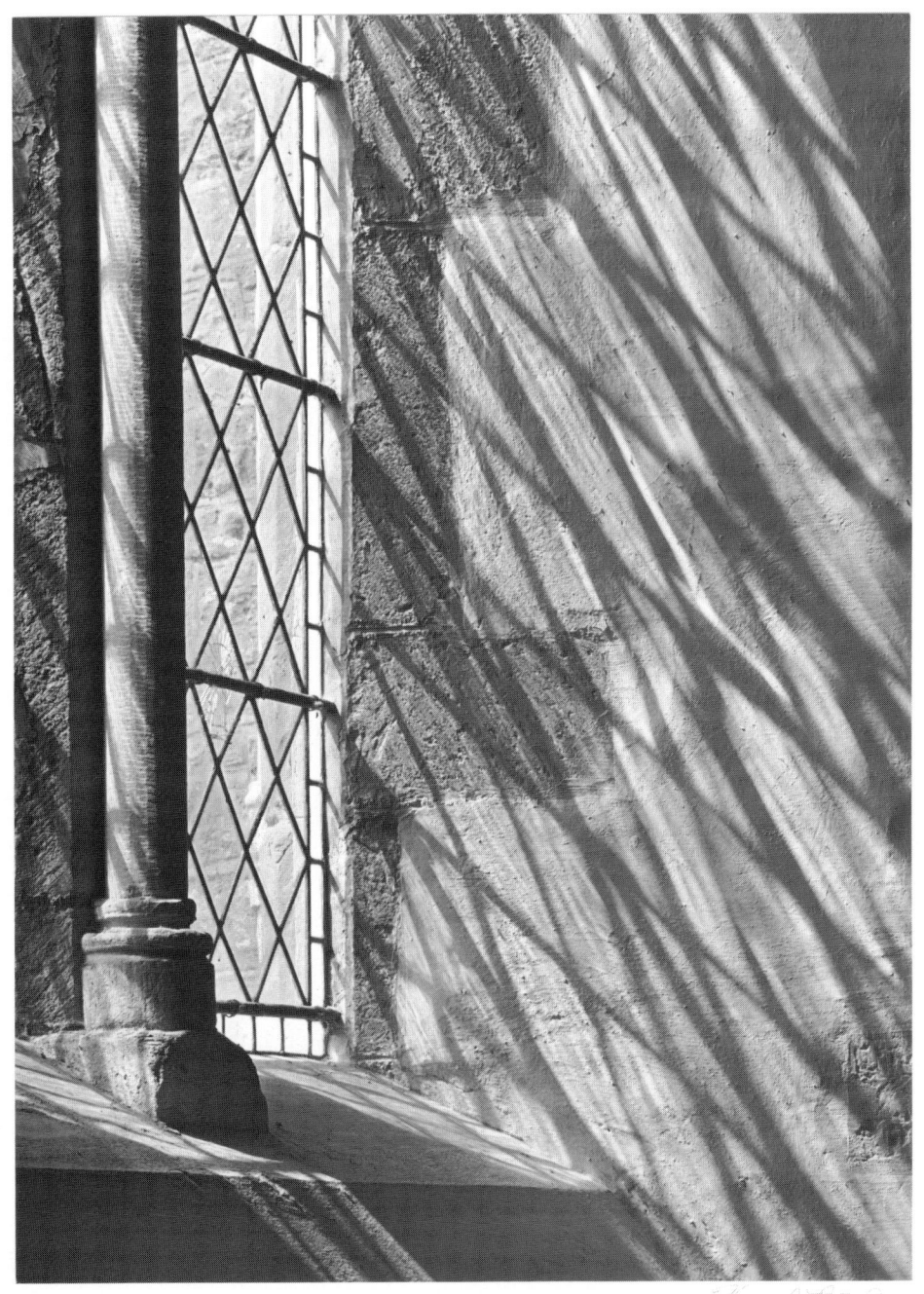

"Window, Woebley," 1982

Silver gelatin print, *Portfolio XIV: English Churches*

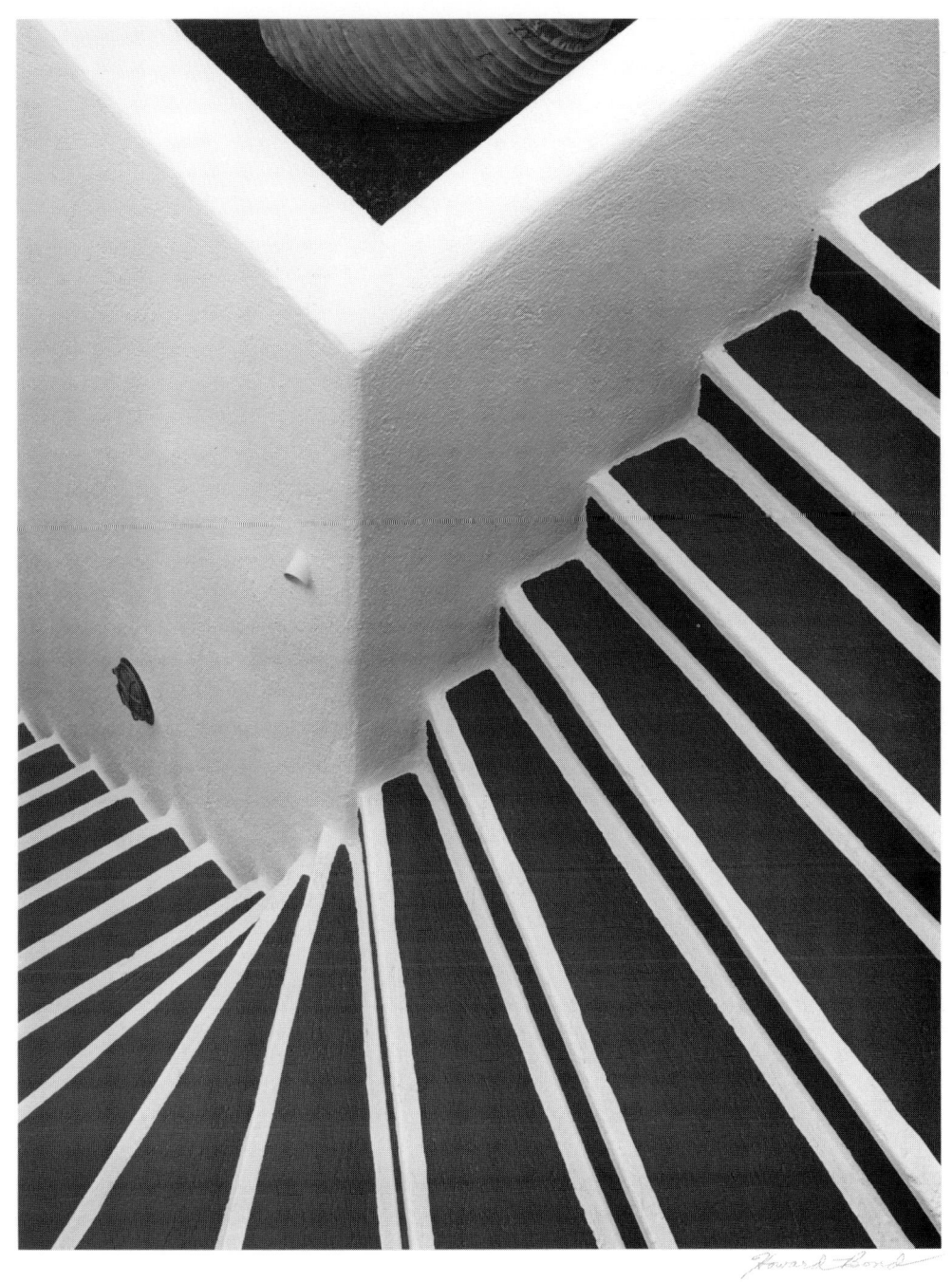

"Pot and Steps, Fira, Santorini," 2004

Silver gelatin print, *Portfolio XXII: Aegean Light*

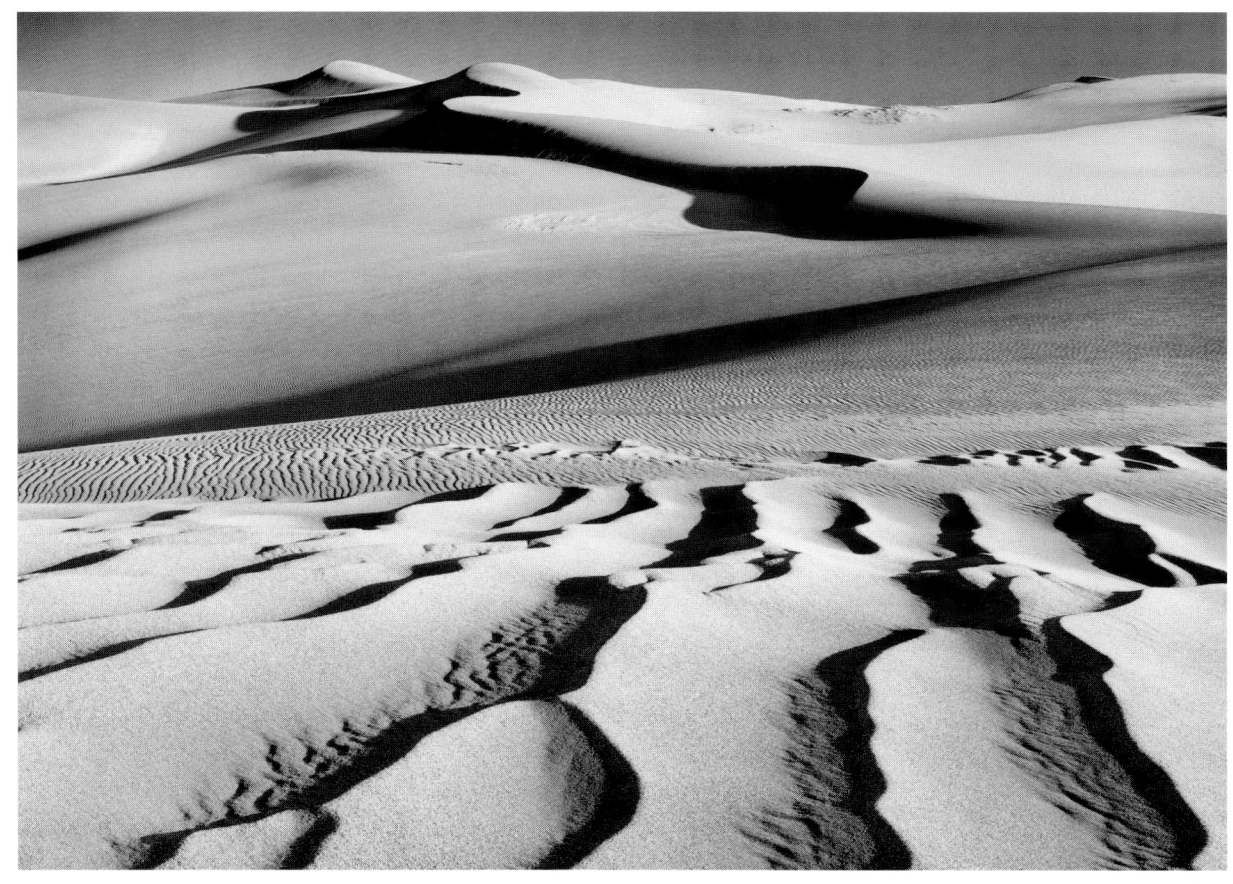

"Wall and Ridges," 1991

Silver gelatin print, *Portfolio XII: Great Sand Dunes*

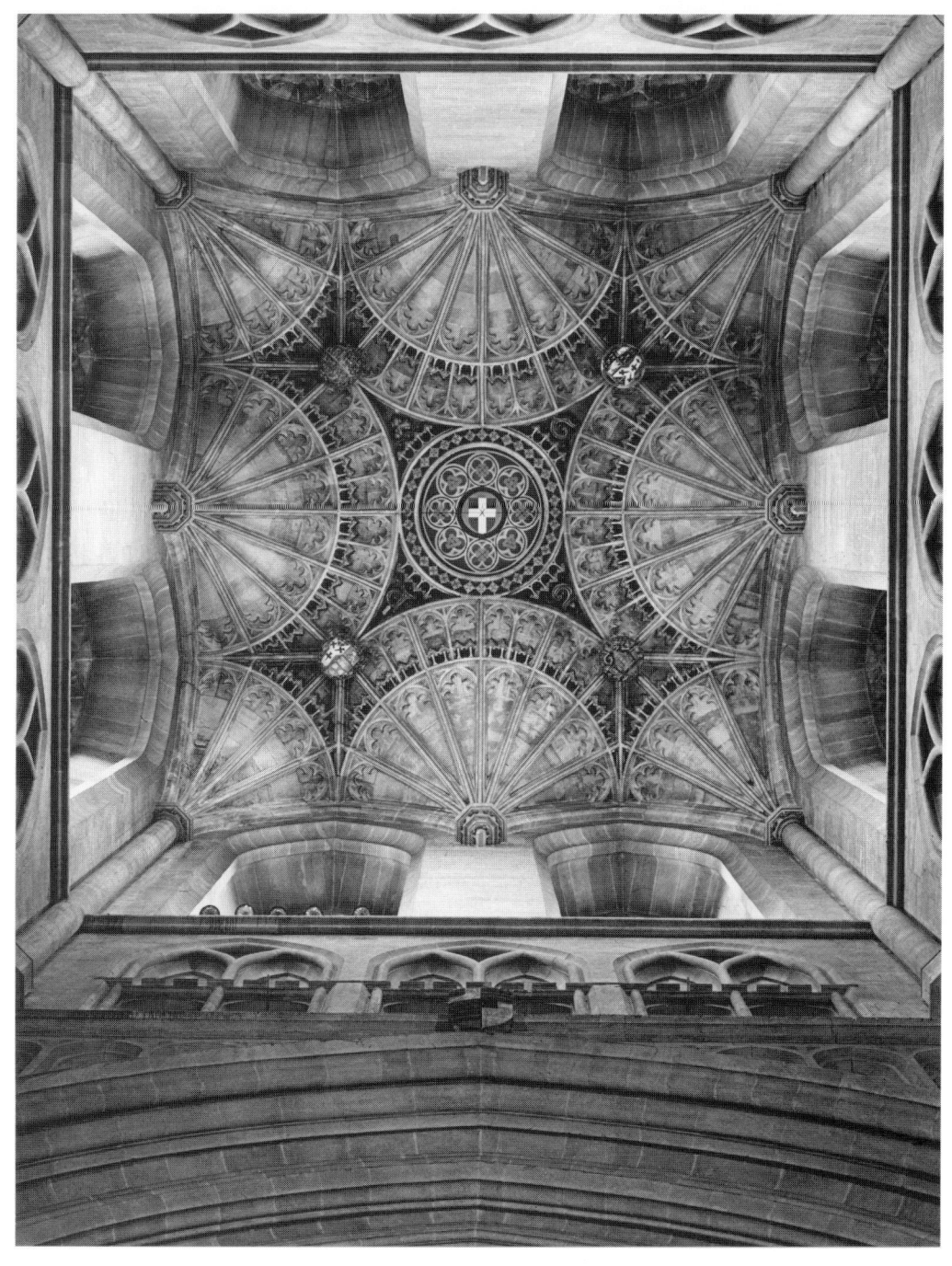

"Central Crossing, Canterbury," 2000
Silver gelatin print, *Portfolio XVIII: Ten Cathedrals*

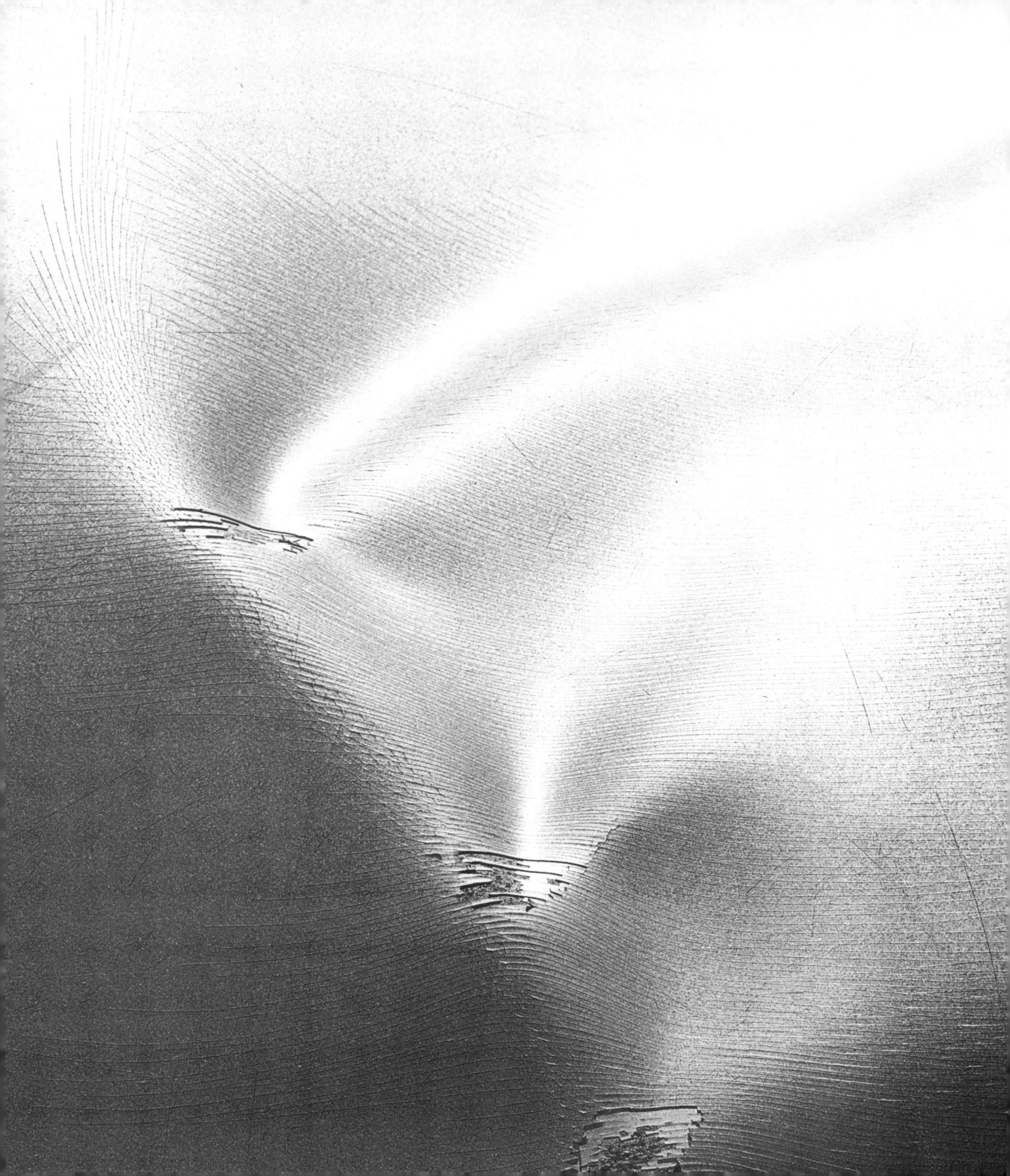

Abstraction

The abstractions found in the Bond portfolios show his exact use of the frame. In *Portfolio VII: Proximity,* he comments, "Two special opportunities for enjoyment often accompany the filling of an entire photograph with a fraction of a subject. Countless details which probably would be overlooked when seeing the original can be savored during leisurely inspection. Perhaps more important, the identity of the subject may not be apparent. Then, if you as the viewer have not been given too much guidance, you will be free to use your imagination and find a personal interpretation of the image."

Often Bond's strongest artistic hand is applied in the darkroom. Halfway through his career he began to alter the tones of his prints using an unsharp mask, a copy of the negative that has been contact printed onto film to create a positive image. The tightly controlled tones range from deep, dark hues to lighter white. The unsharp mask creates a separation between tones that lie next to each other, allowing more detail to emerge. In many of his images, tonal variations help to create bold shapes and exaggerated lines, further precluding the photograph's function as a mere record of the subject that once appeared before the photographer's lens.

In this selection of abstracted images the viewer will find well-weathered objects. Sand and water move, struck by light and wind, while metal and rock display their rough-cut faces. Bond's artistry alters these objects, creating mesmerizing forms that engage our imaginations.

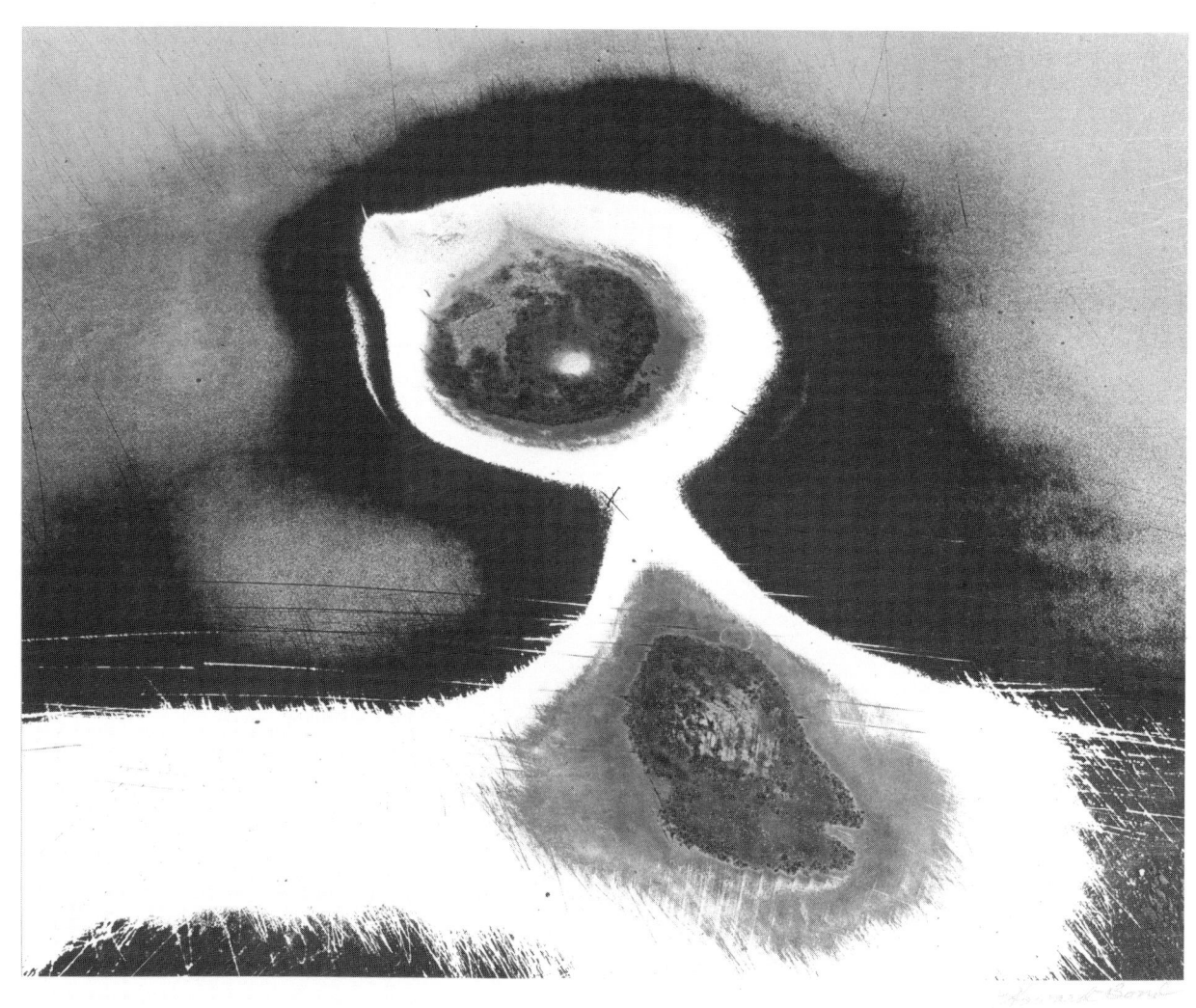

"Roof, Colorado," 1990

Silver gelatin print, *Portfolio XX: Abstraction*

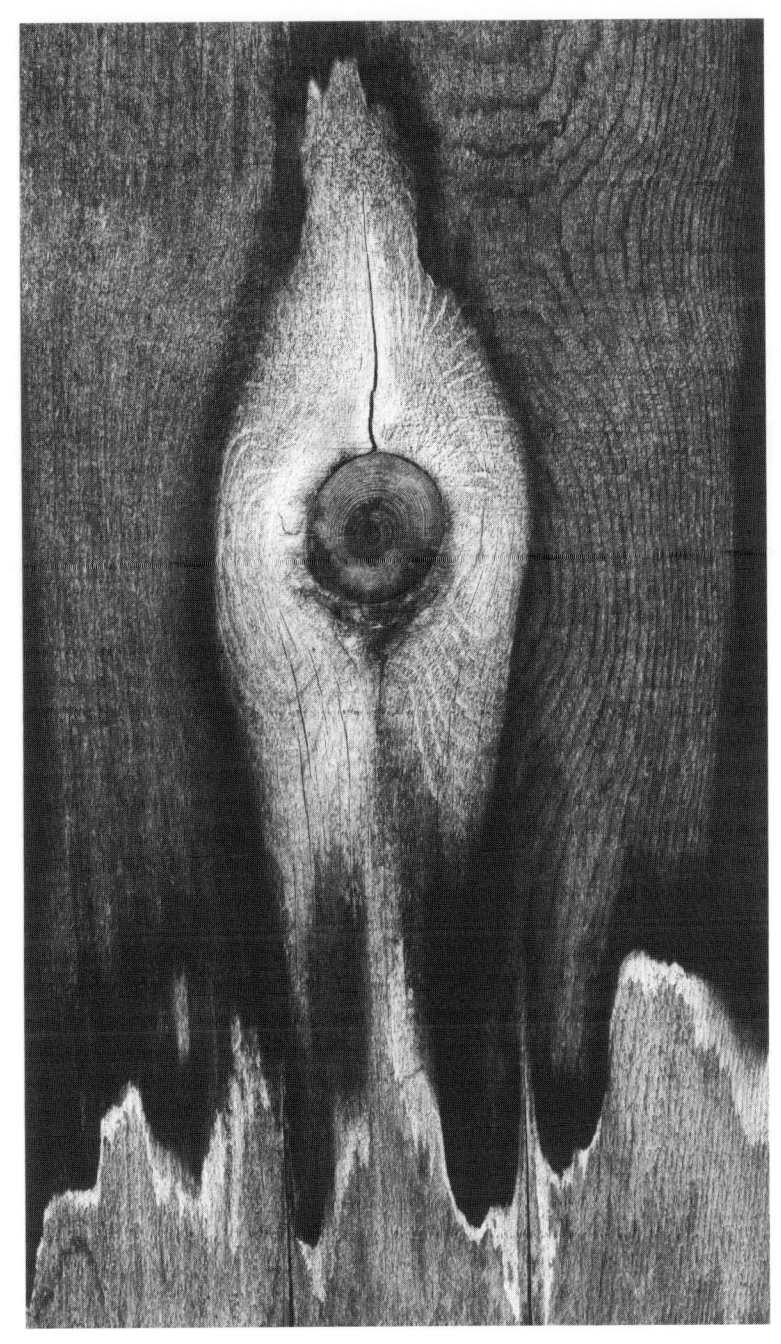

"Water Pattern," 1976

Silver gelatin print, *Portfolio X: Contact Prints*

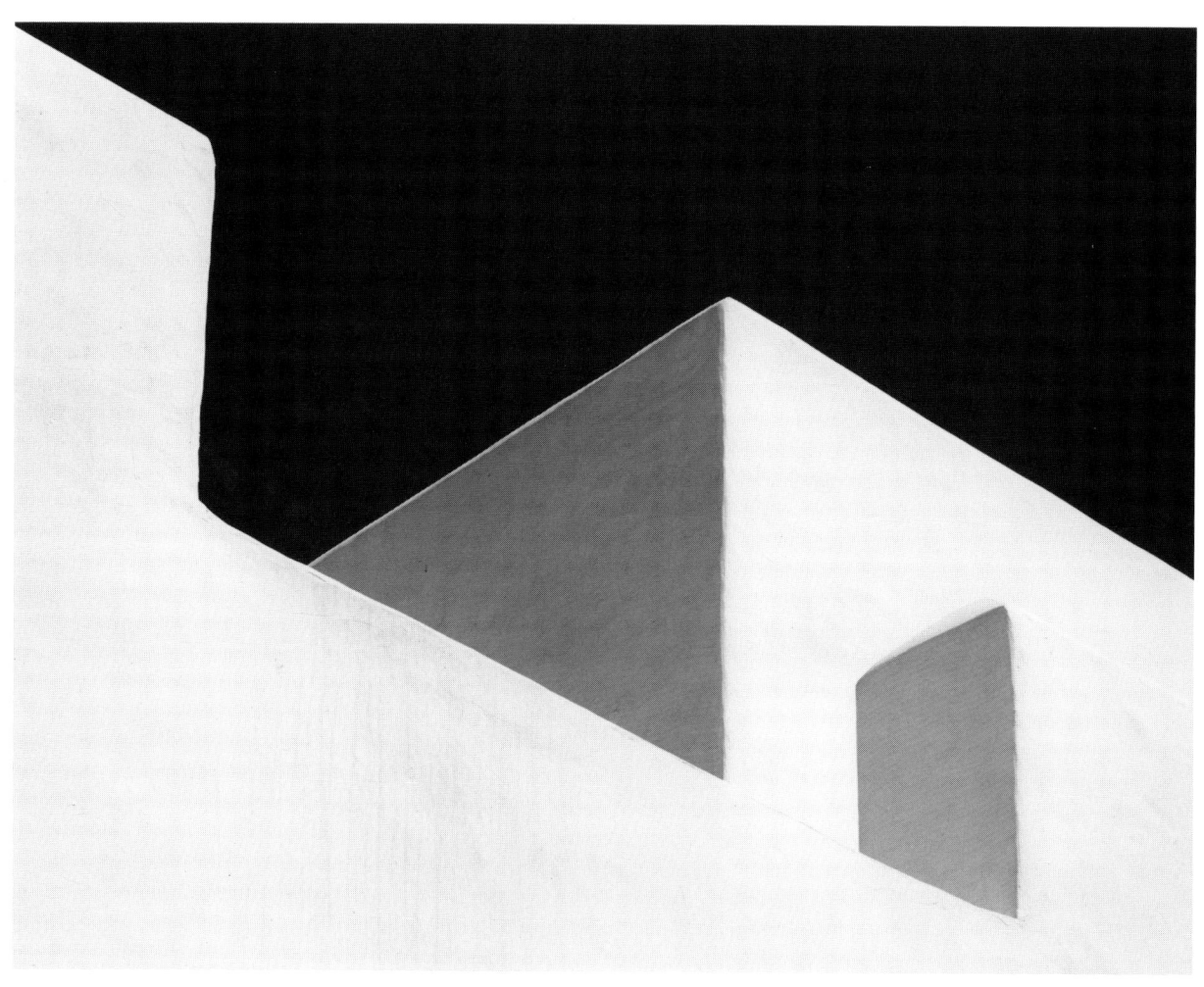

"Rectilinear, Naoussa, Paros," 2004

Silver gelatin print, *Portfolio XXII: Aegean Light*

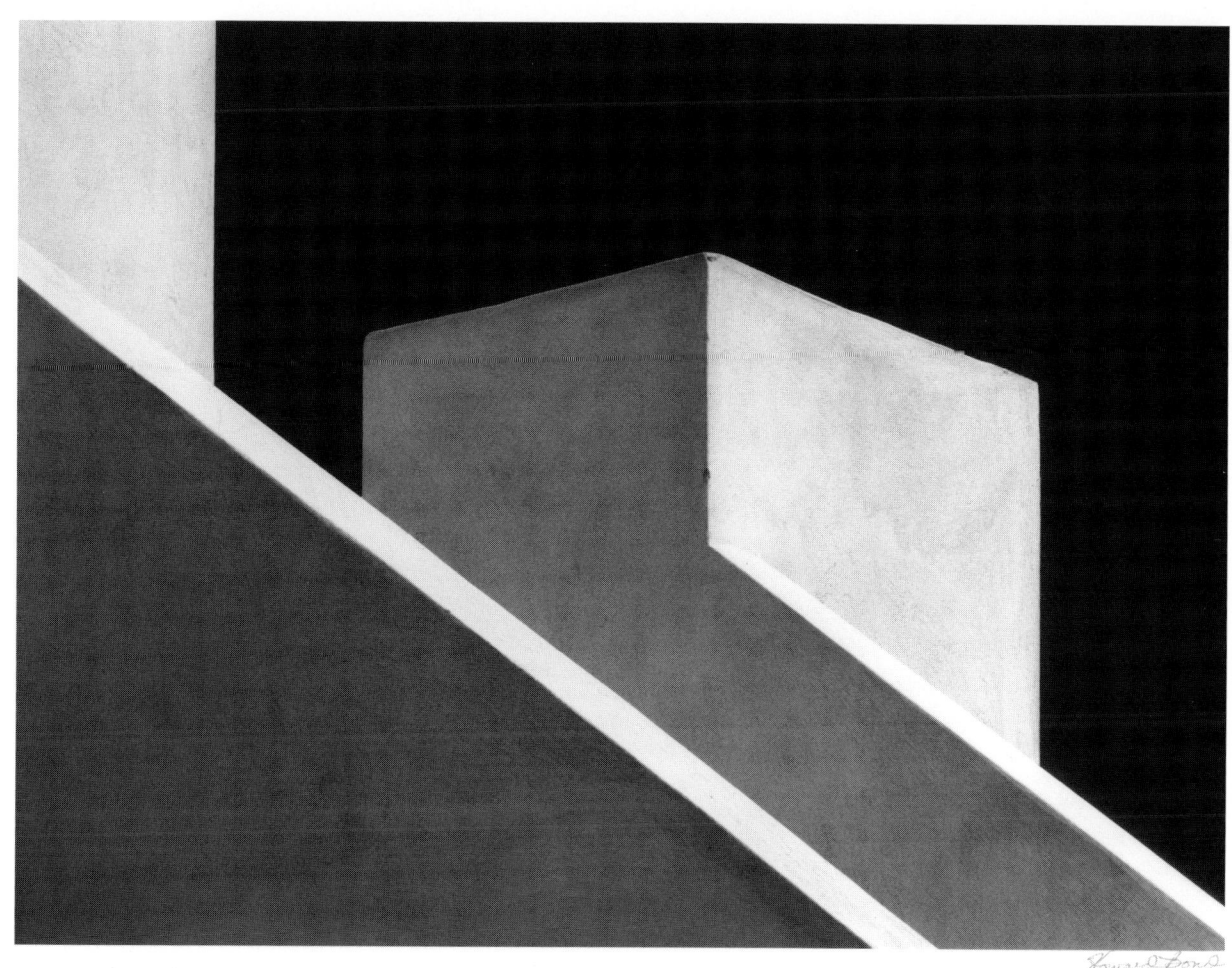

"Blockhouse, Ios," 1987

Silver gelatin print, *Portfolio XI: White Motif*

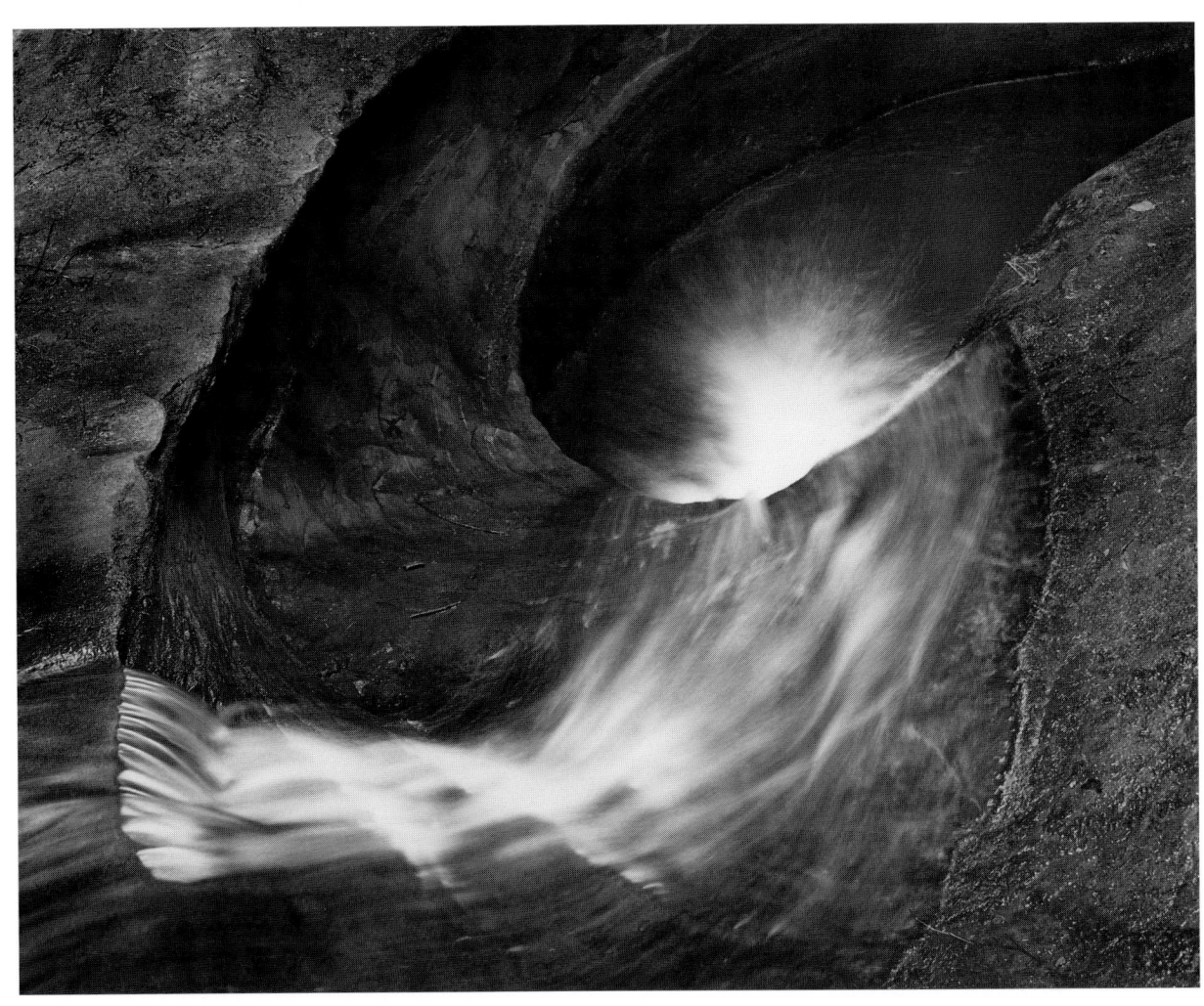

"Devil's Bathtub, Hocking Hills, Ohio," 1997

Silver gelatin print, *Portfolio XVI: 1990s Landscapes*

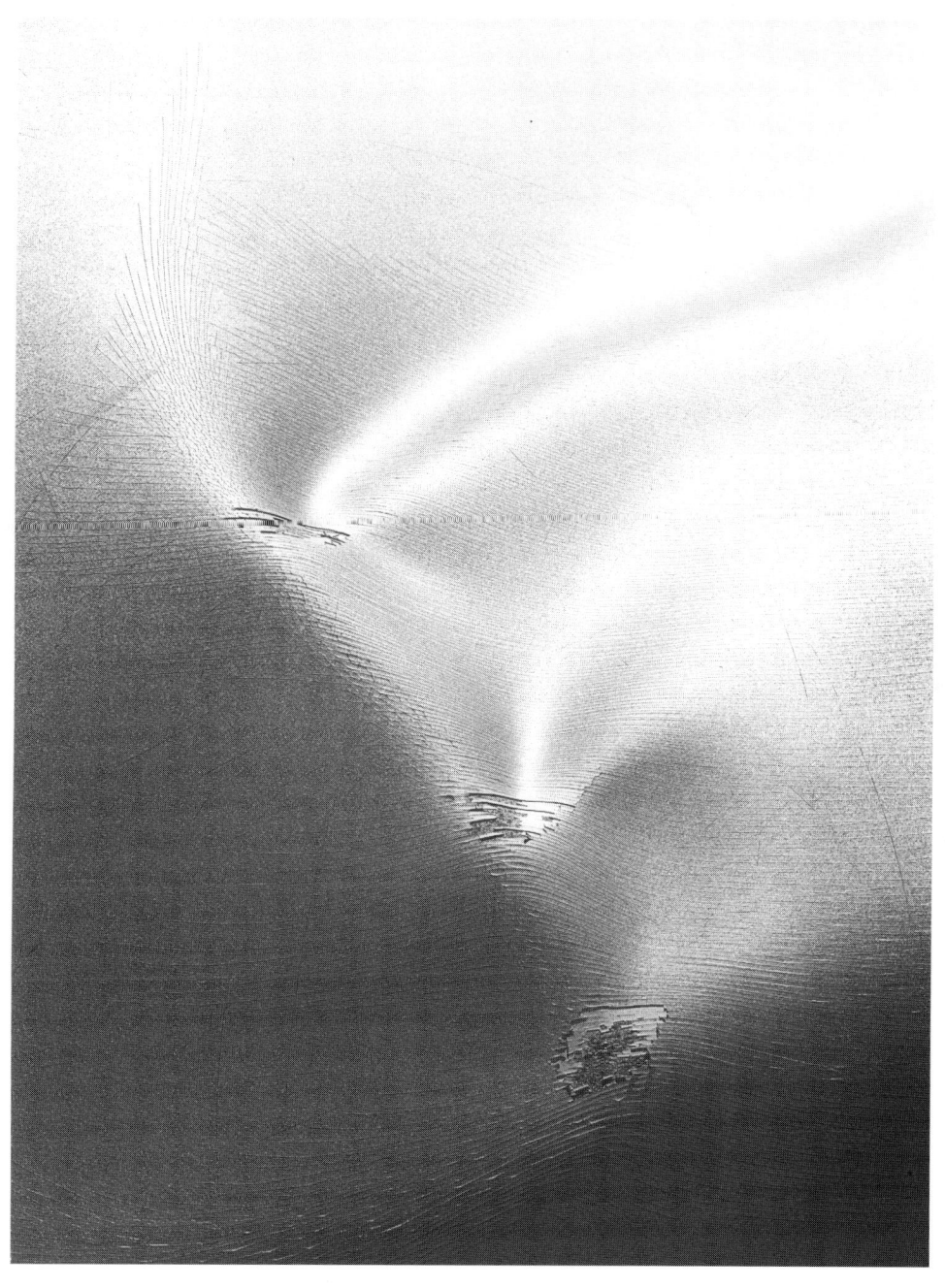

"Nixon Auto Parts No. 18, Michigan," 1986

Silver gelatin print, *Portfolio XX: Abstraction*

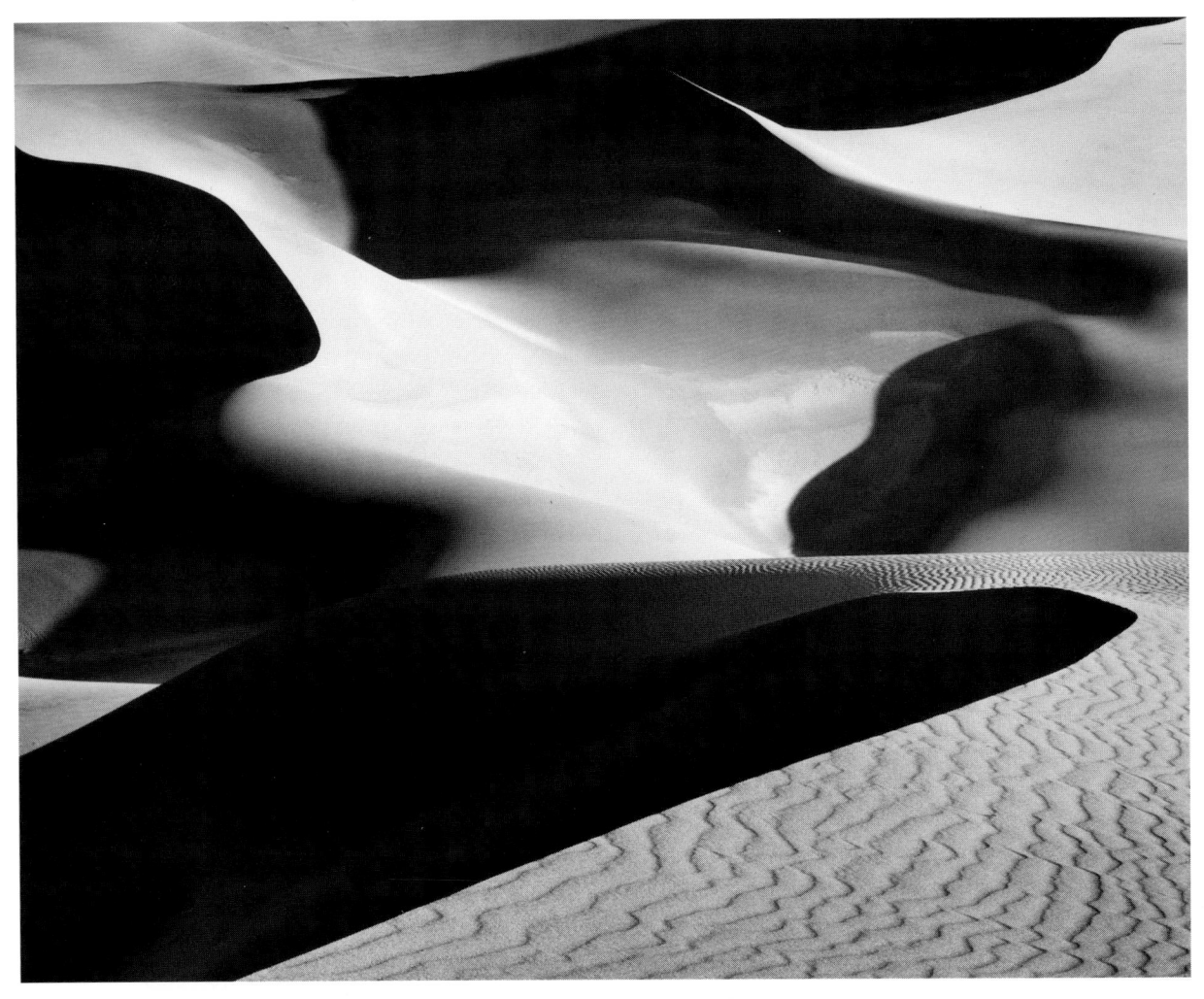

"Dunes II," 1990

Silver gelatin print, *Portfolio XII: Great Sand Dunes*

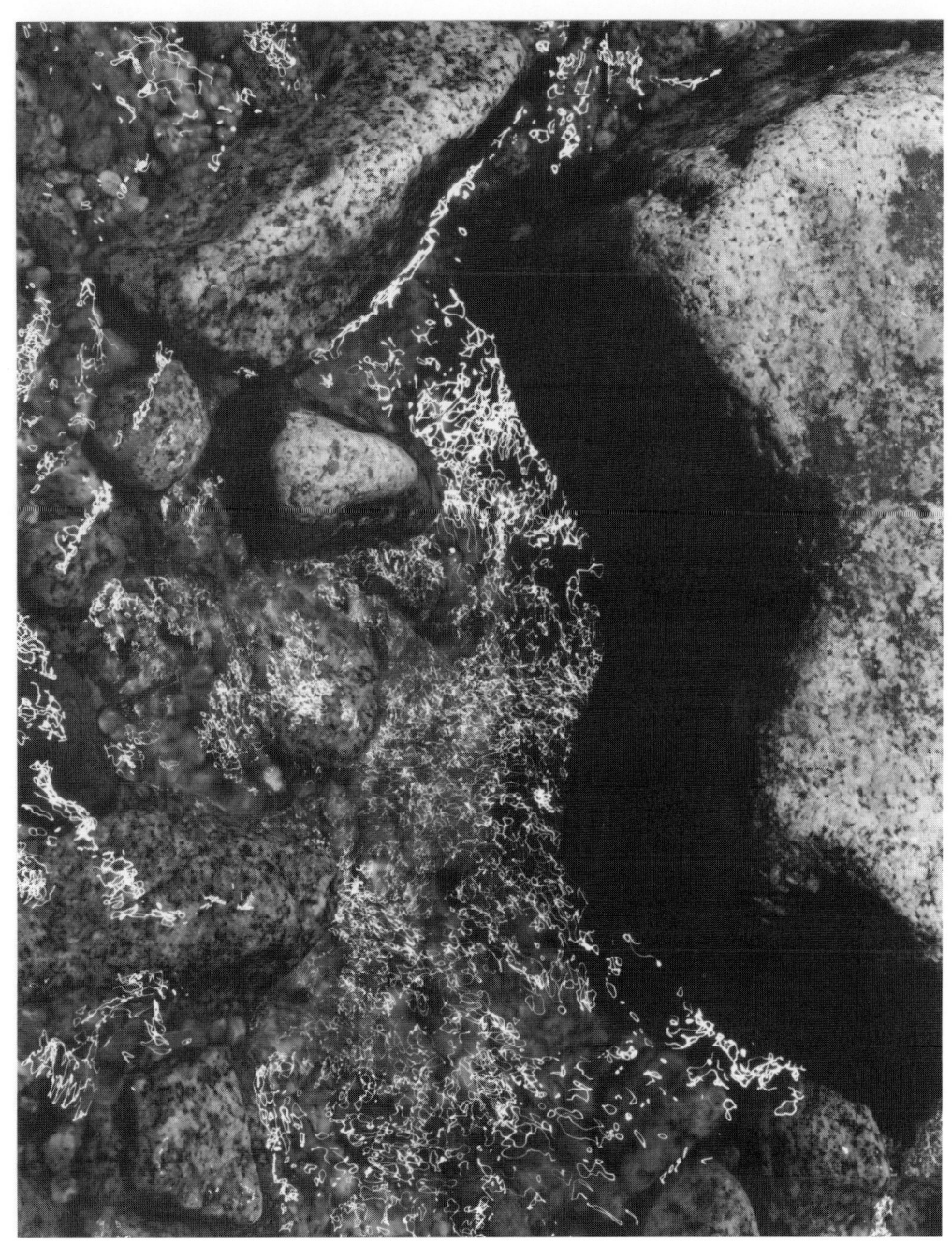

"Detail, South Fork Kings River," 1972

Silver gelatin print, *Portfolio I: Kings Canyon*

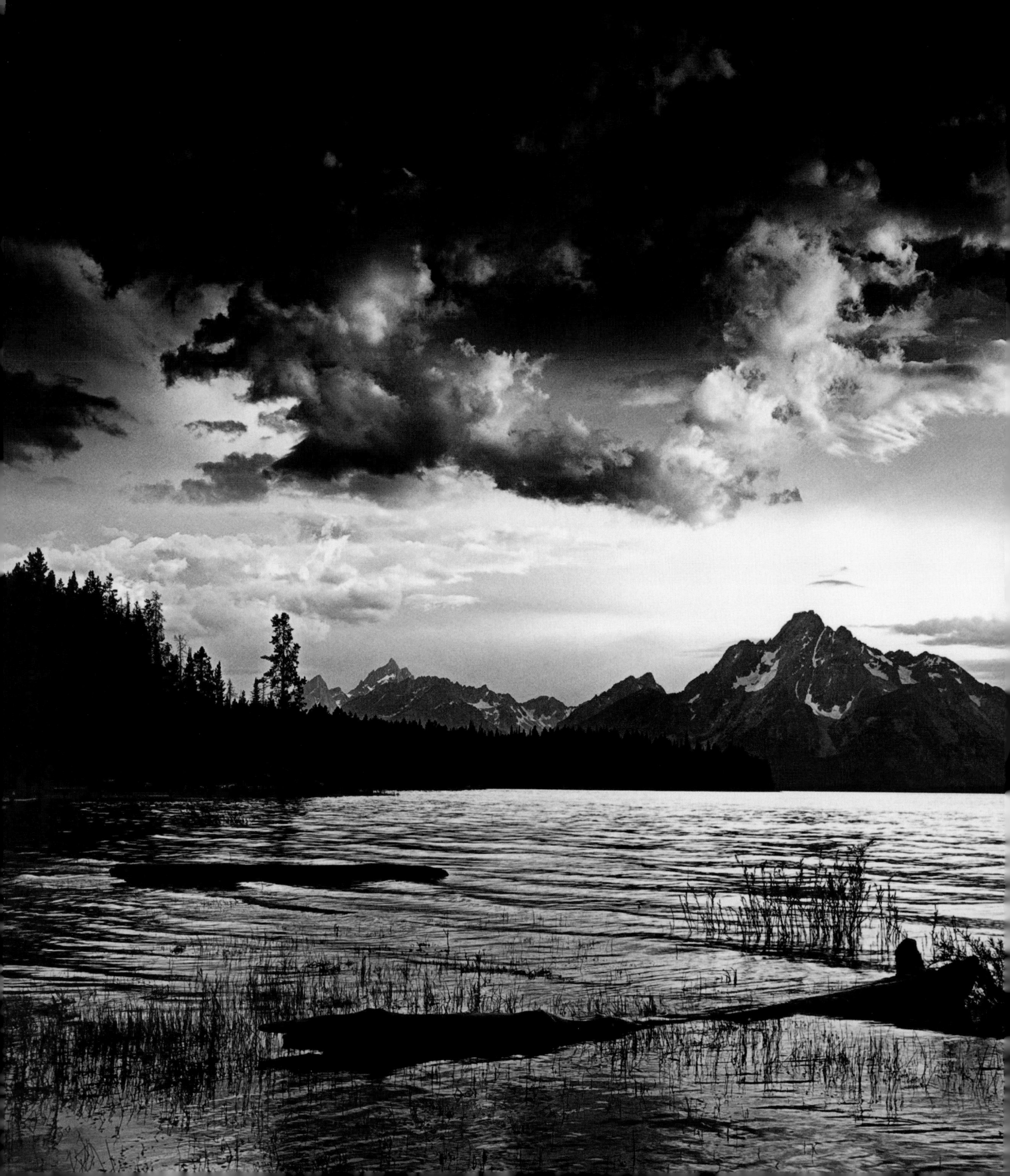

Place

Landscapes and people from throughout the world appear in Bond's portfolios. This selection includes "Twilight, Jackson Lake, Wyoming" (1968) and "Thunderstorm and Tree, Wyoming" (1981), both reminiscent of the grand landscapes of Bond's mentor Ansel Adams. Bond's rare photographs of people seem to belong among his landscapes as explorations of the human body in various physical settings.

A strikingly beautiful image entitled "Mountain Stream" (1976) is unlike any other Bond photograph. In it a woman lies submerged and enveloped by cascades of water. Her dark hair spreads behind her, flowing along with the movement of the stream, matching the movement of the water across the rocks above her. She is centered in the composition, but her image is obscured, an abstracted effect achieved by a long exposure, which allowed the photographer to capture the movement of water while blurring the subject.

"Hawaiian Barber" (1973) is also unique. In this straightforward image Bond has captured a barber, reclining with bare feet up. Around him, instead of a natural setting, is the landscape of his shop, with its shelves, brooms, fan, bottles, cash register, and mirror reflecting what lies behind the camera.

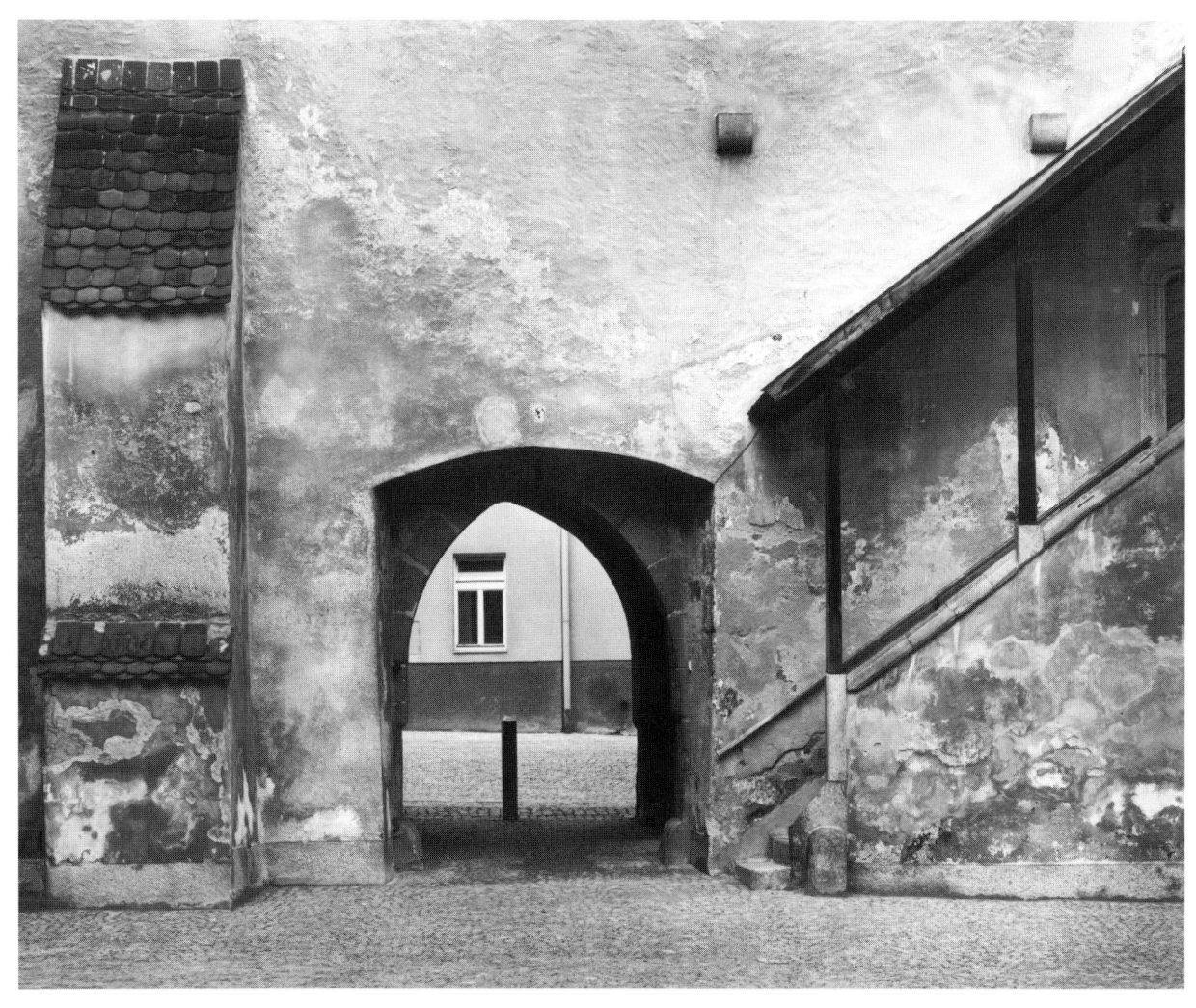

"Palace Courtyard, Freistadt," 1978

Silver gelatin print, *Portfolio II: Austria*

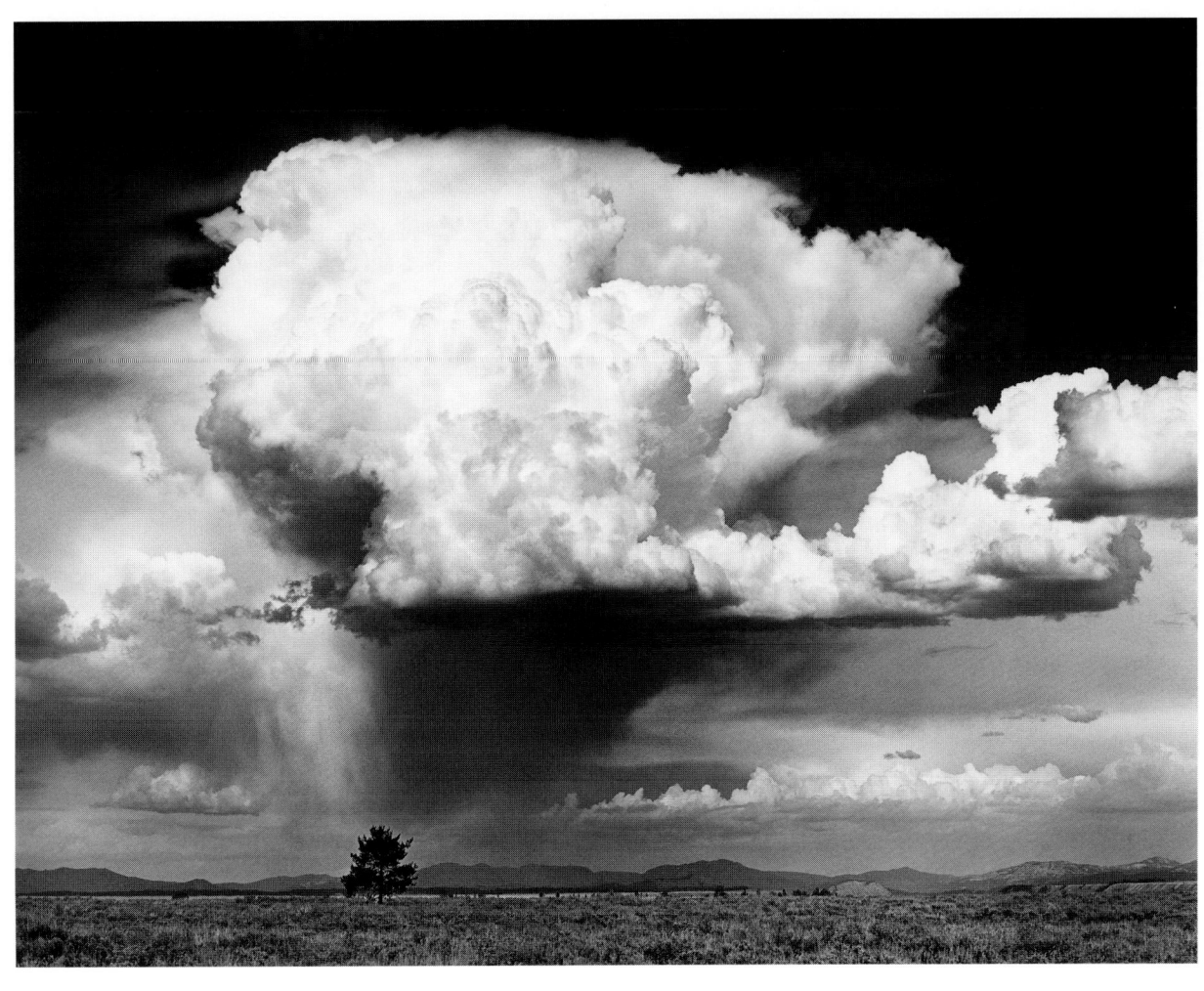

"Thunderstorm and Tree, Wyoming," 1981

Silver gelatin print, *Portfolio XIII: Photographs in Four Decades*

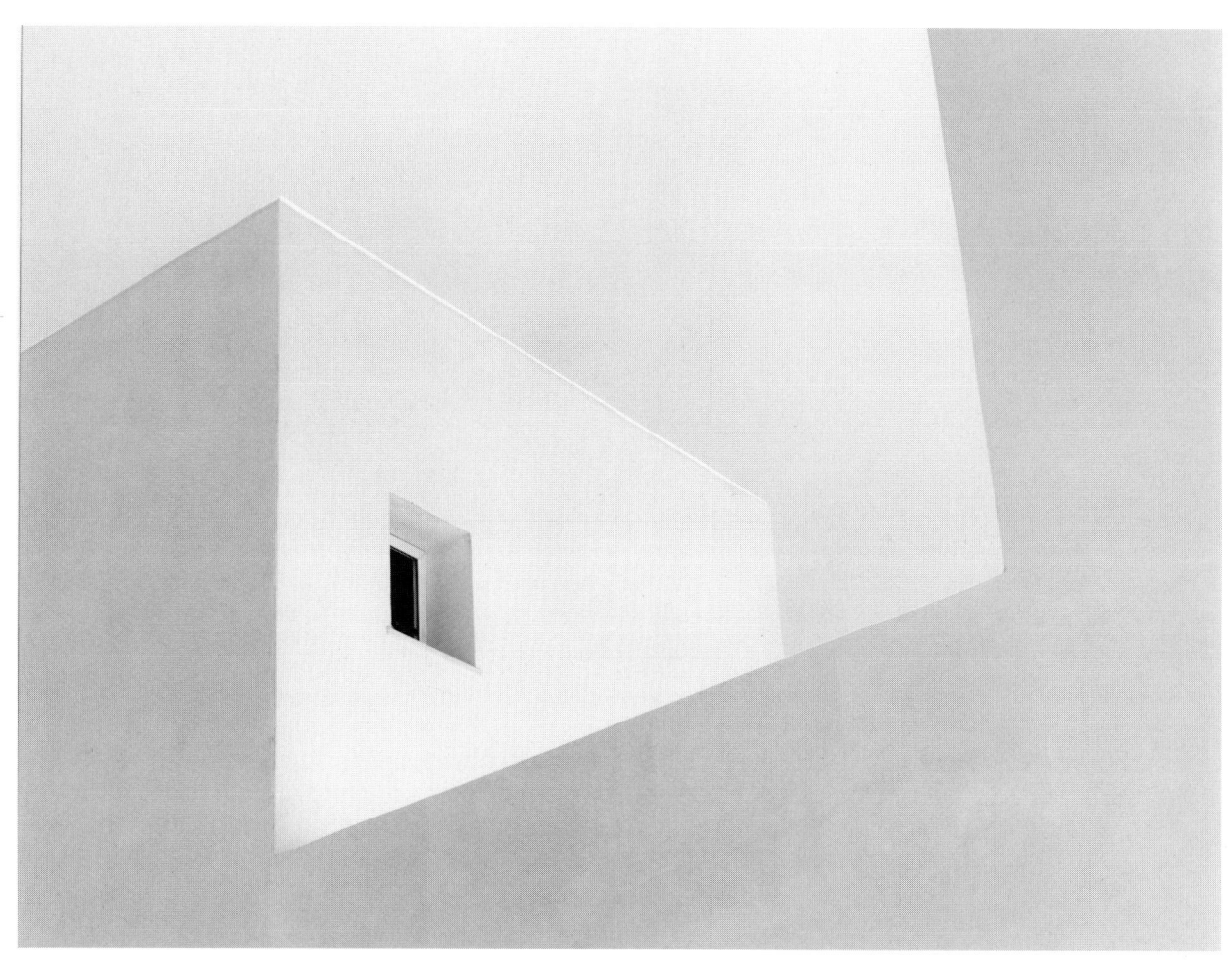

"Light and Dark, Ios," 2004

Silver gelatin print, *Portfolio XXII: Aegean Light*

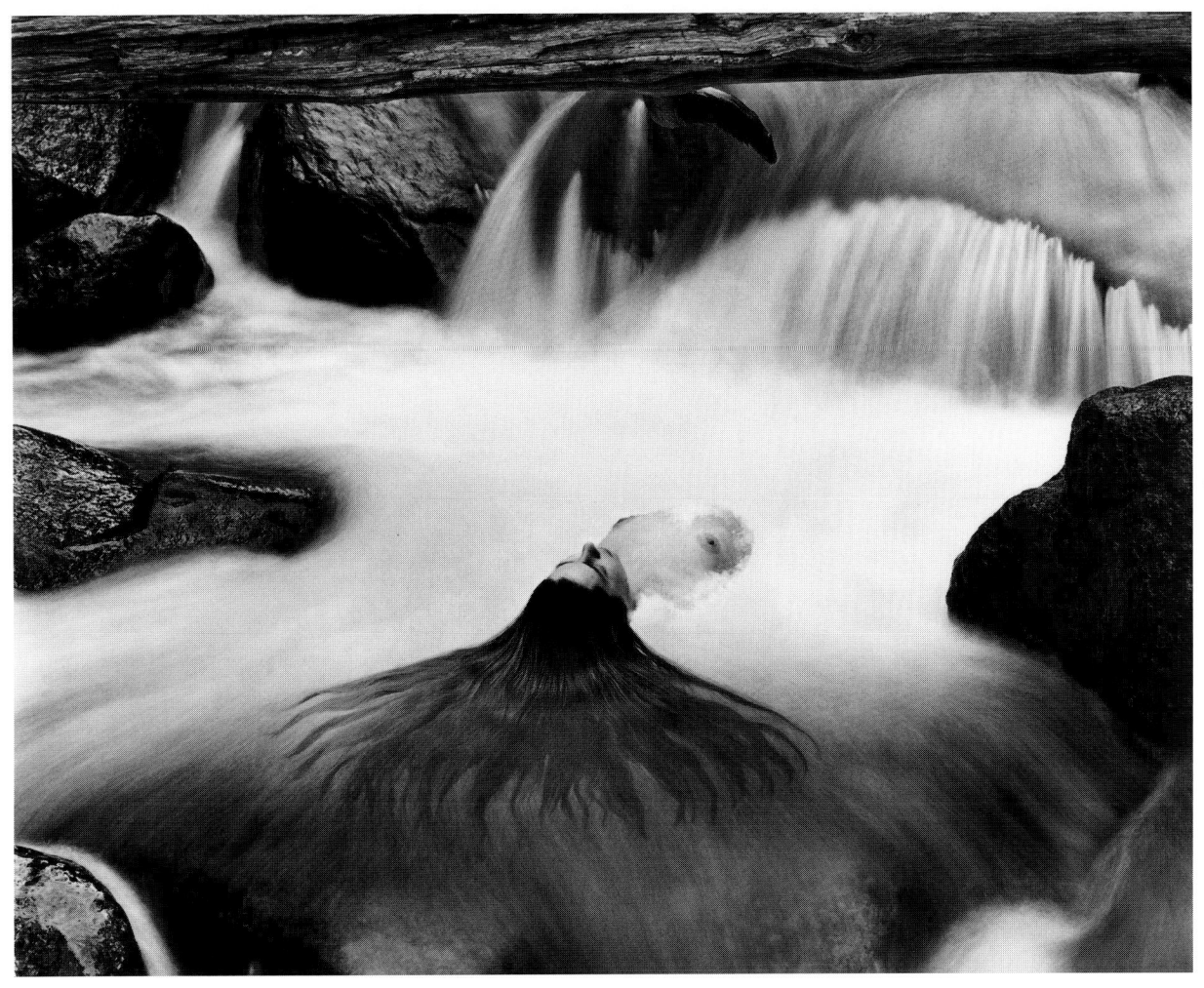

"Mountain Stream," 1976

Silver gelatin print, *Portfolio XIII: Photographs in Four Decades*

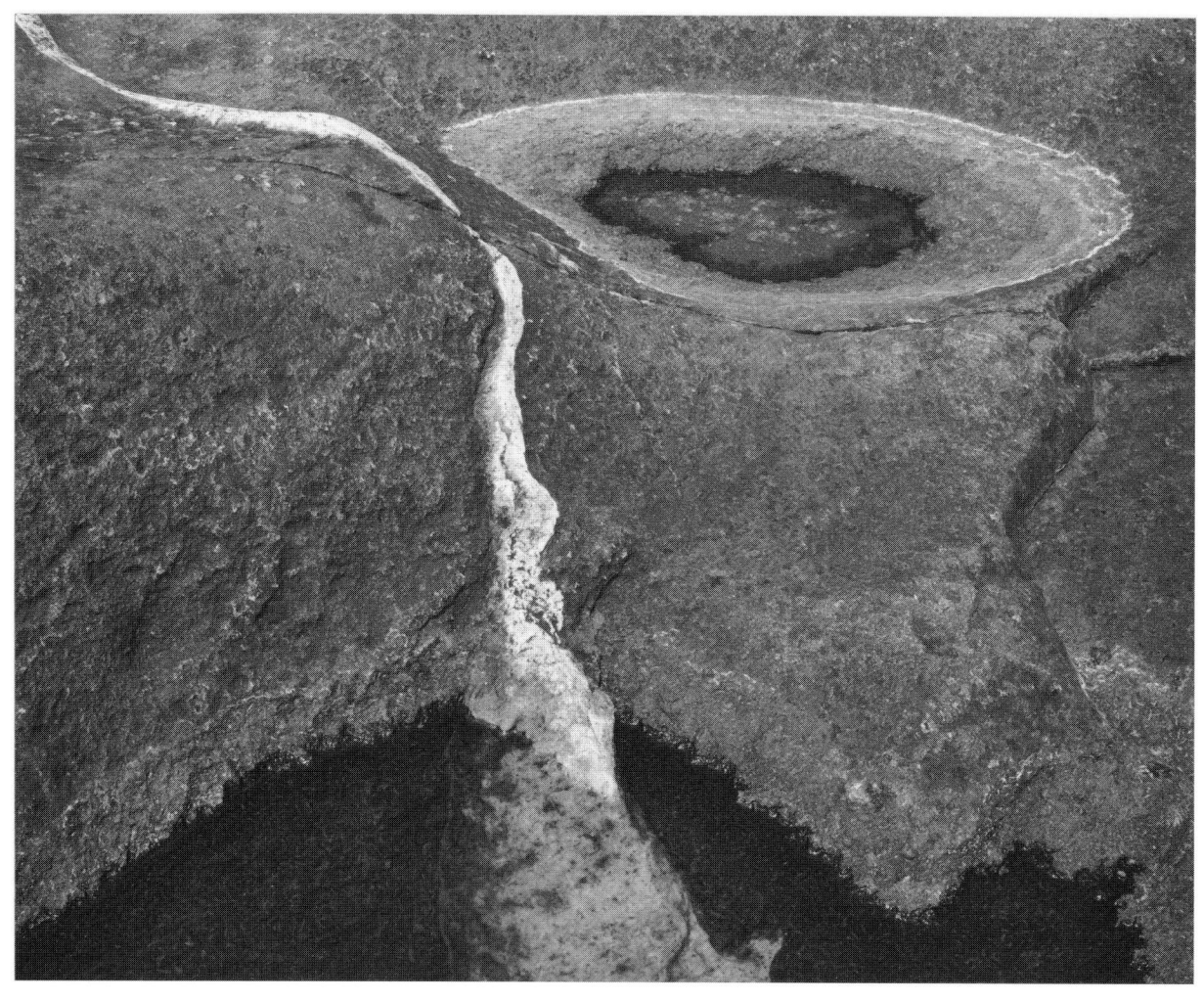

"Solid/Liquid, Lake Superior Provincial Park," 1988

Silver gelatin print, *Portfolio IX: Ontario*

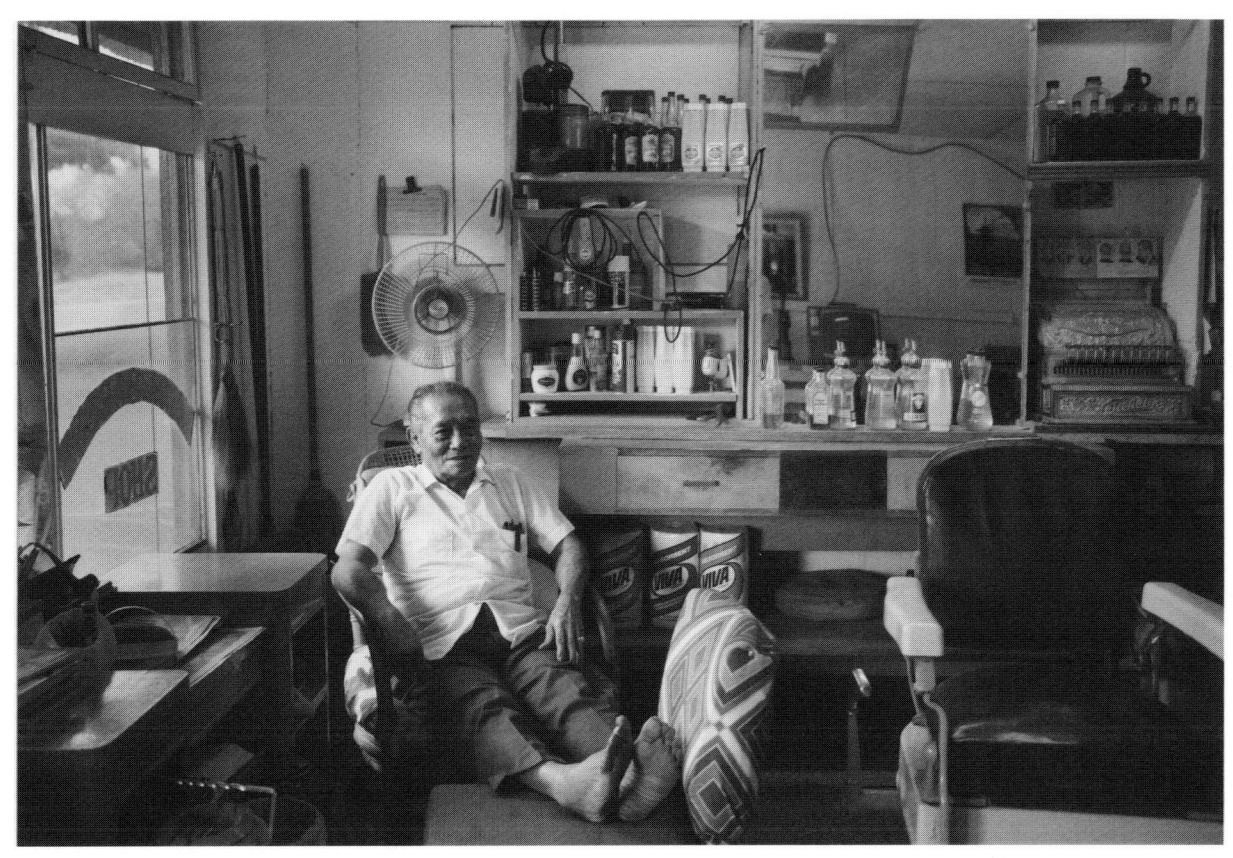

"Hawaiian Barber," 1973

Silver gelatin print, *Portfolio VIII: People and Places*

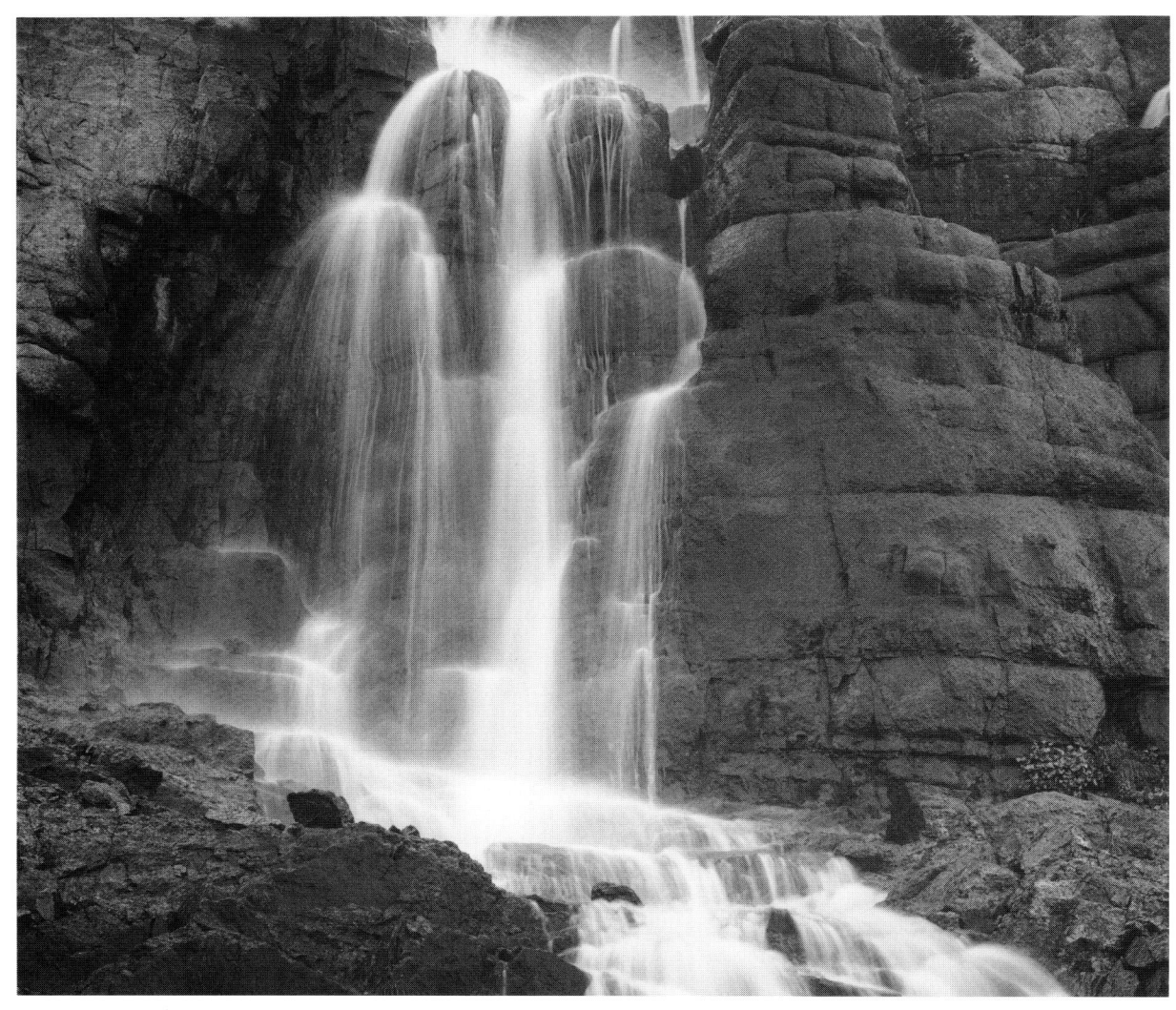

"Needleton Creek Falls, Chicago Basin," 1982

Silver gelatin print, *Portfolio V: Colorado*

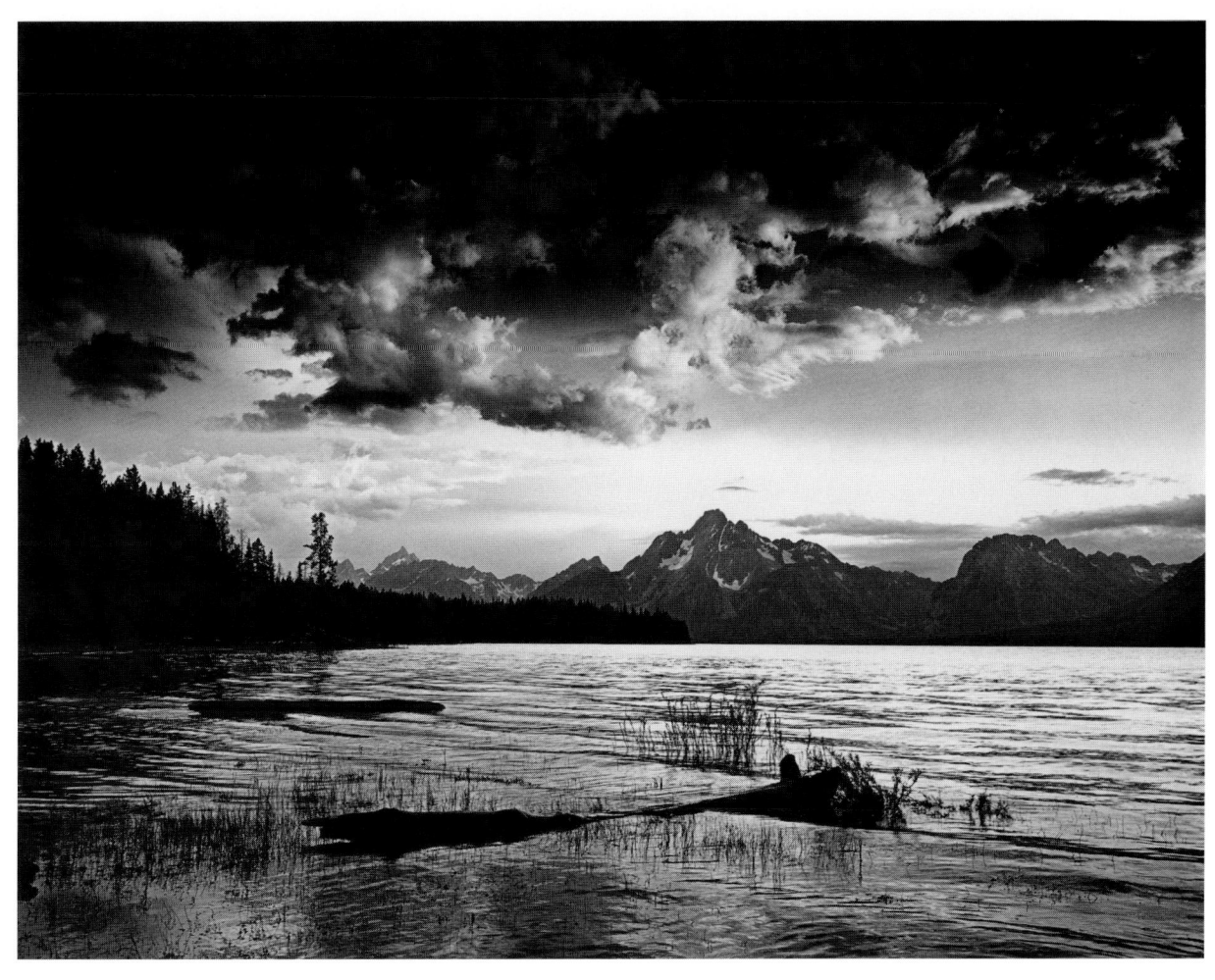

"Twilight, Jackson Lake, Wyoming," 1968

Silver gelatin print, *Portfolio XIII: Photographs in Four Decades*

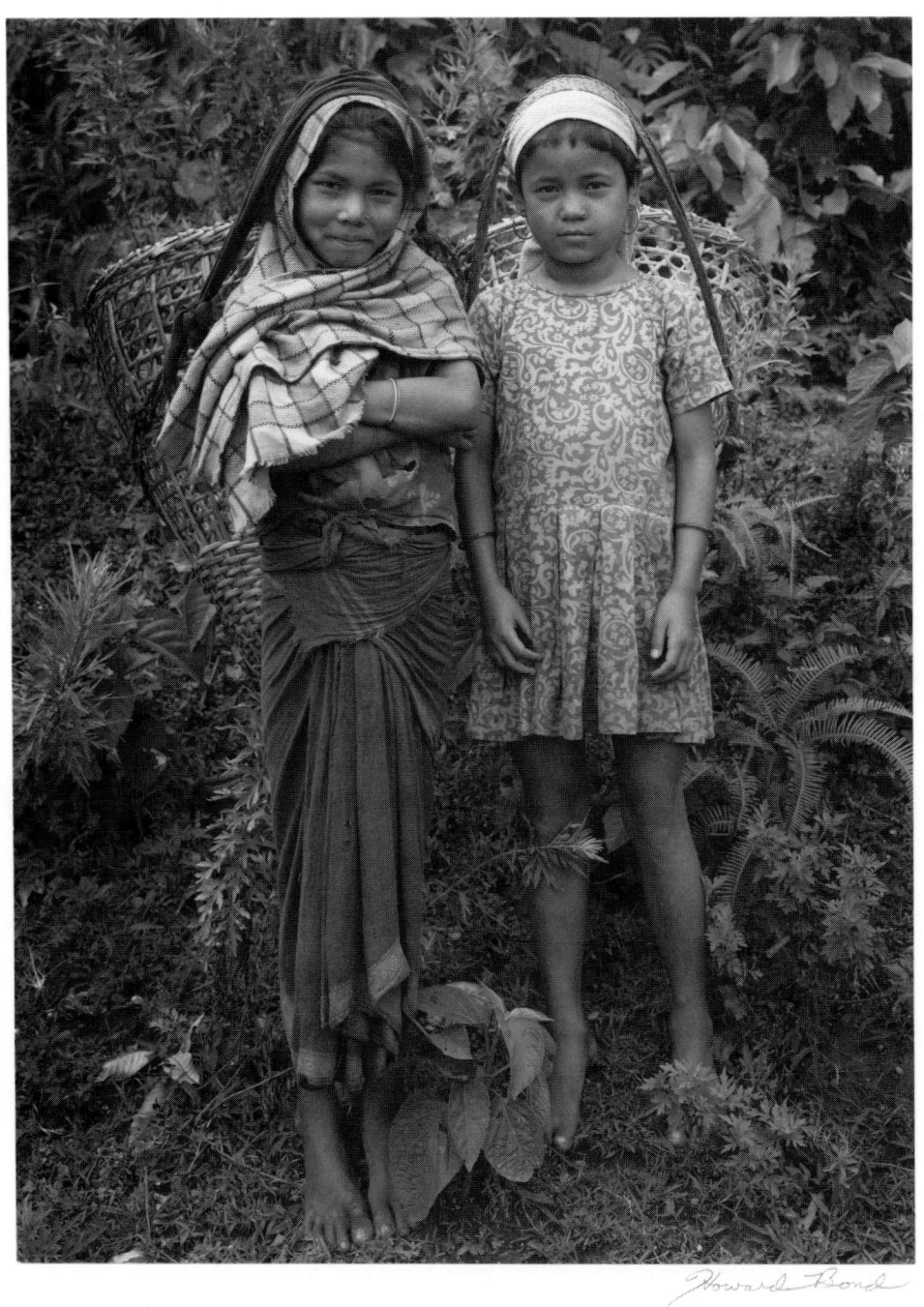

"Going to Market, Pokhara, Nepal," 1973

Silver gelatin print, *Portfolio VIII: People and Places*

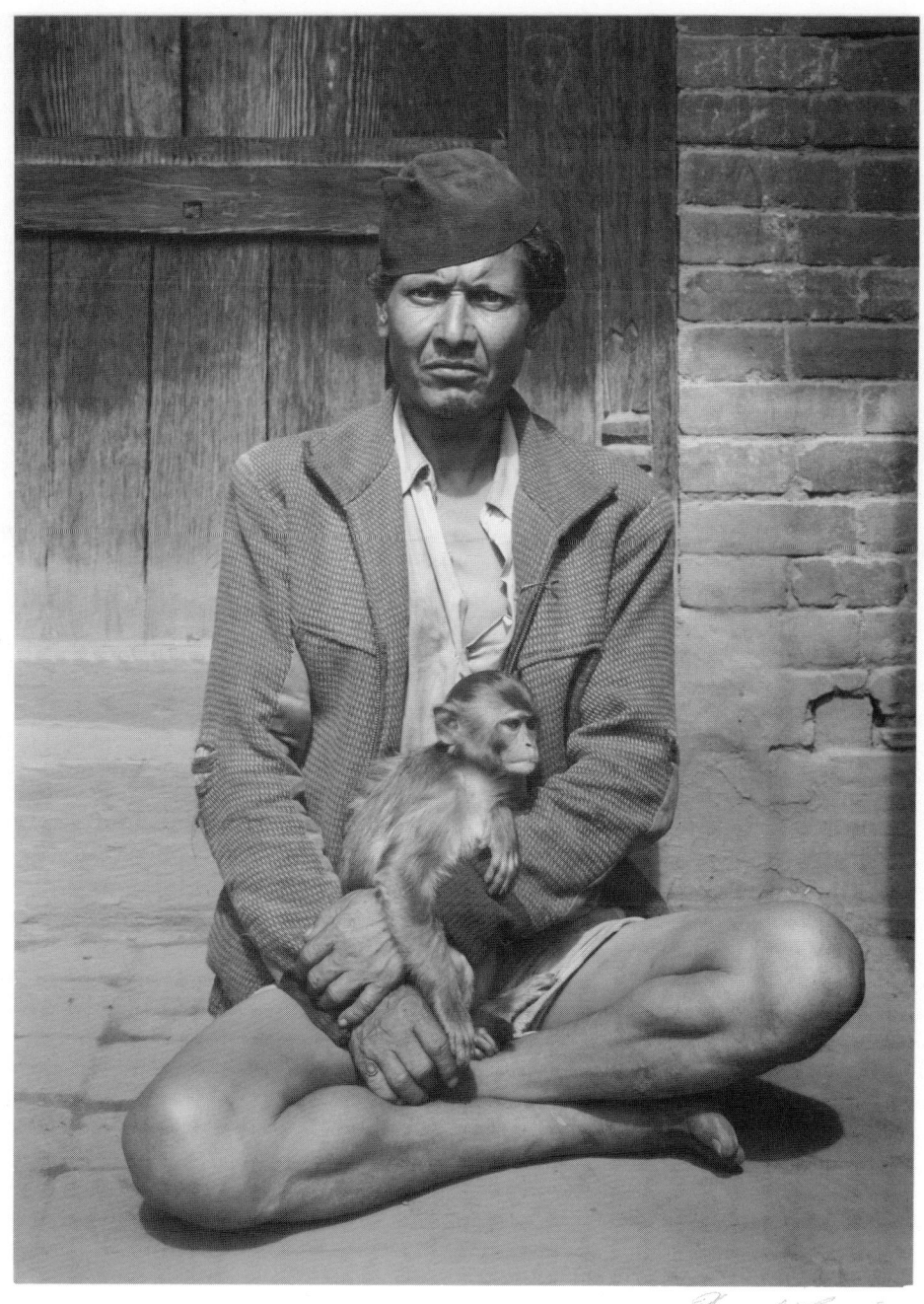

"Neighborhood Jester, Katmandu, Nepal," 1973

Silver gelatin print, *Portfolio VIII: People and Places*

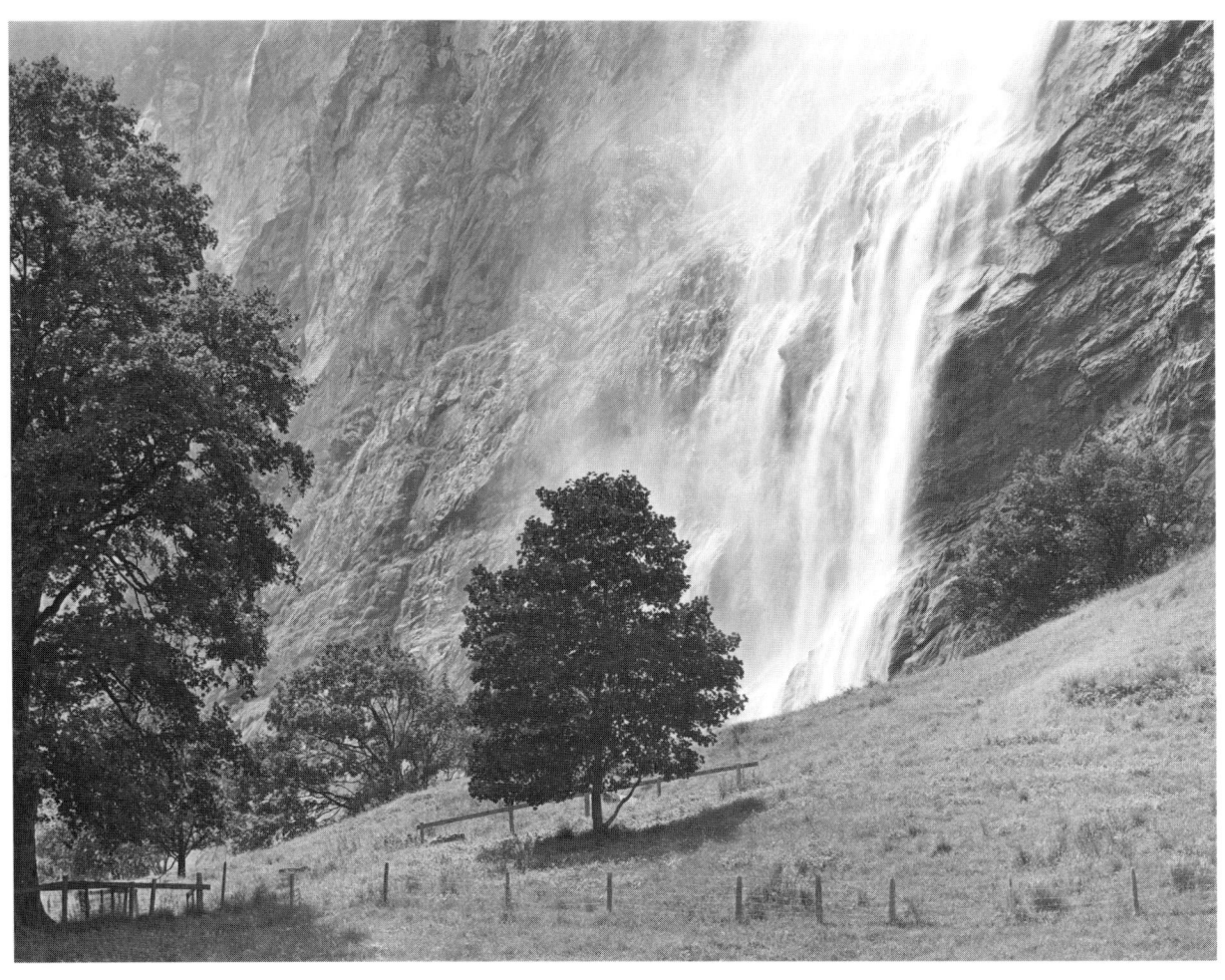

"Waterfall, Lauterbrunnen," 2001

Silver gelatin print, *Portfolio XXI: Alps*

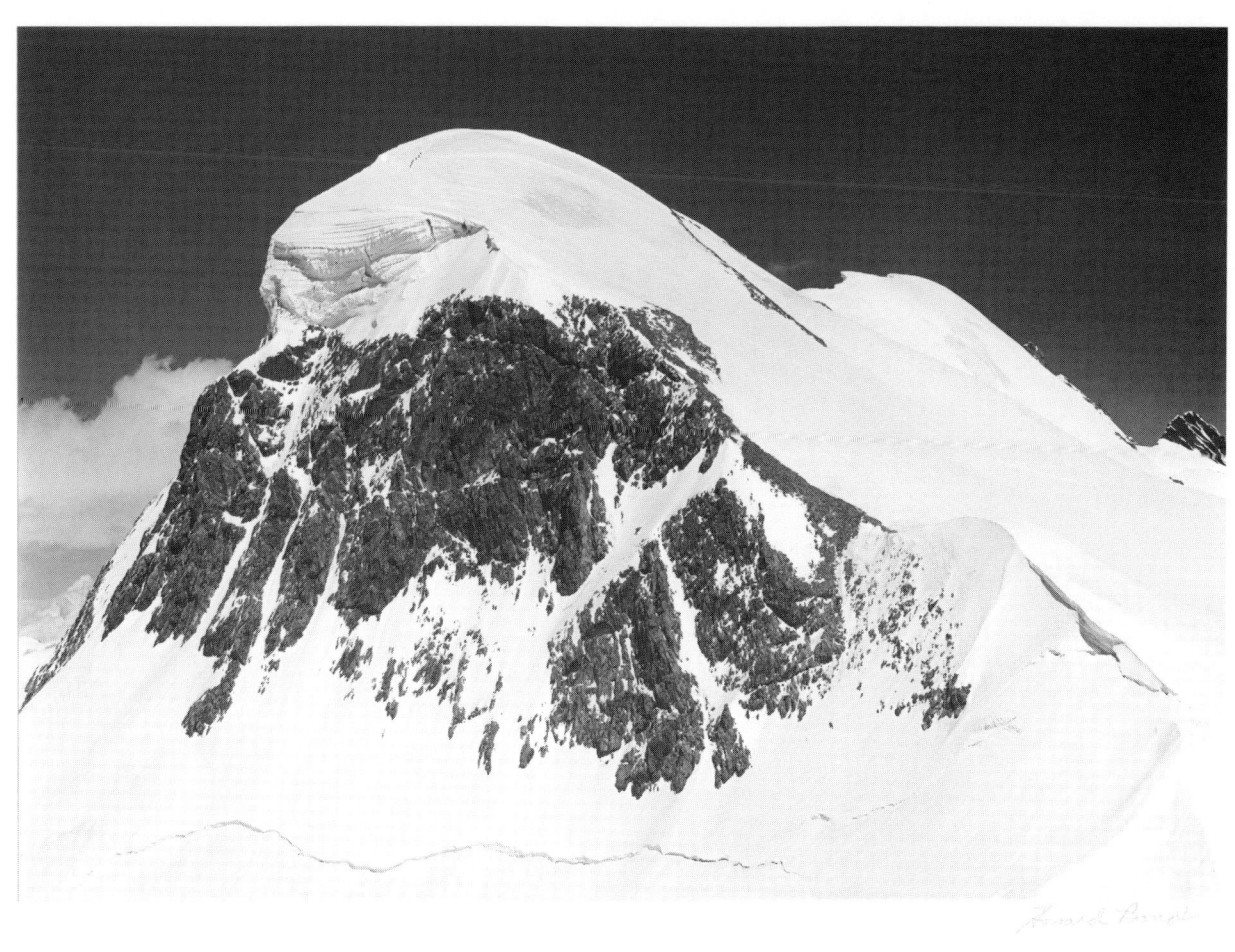

"Six Climbers on the Breithorn," 2001

Silver gelatin print, *Portfolio XXI: Alps*

The Portfolios of
HOWARD BOND

Portfolio I: *Kings Canyon, 1974*

Portfolio II: *Austria, 1979*

Portfolio III: *Victor, 1980*

Portfolio IV: *Huron River, 1982*

Portfolio V: *Colorado, 1985*

Portfolio VI: *Greek Islands, 1985*

Portfolio VII: *Proximity, 1987*

Portfolio VIII: *People and Places, 1987*

Portfolio IX: *Ontario, 1989*

Portfolio X: *Contact Prints, 1990*

Portfolio XI: *White Motif, 1991*

Portfolio XII: *Great Sand Dunes , 1992*

Portfolio XIII: *Photographs in Four Decades, 1994*

Portfolio XIV: *English Churches, 1996*

Portfolio XV: *Bristlecone Pines, 1997*

Portfolio XVI: *1990s Landscapes, 1999*

Portfolio XVII: *New Zealand, 2000*

Portfolio XVIII: *Ten Cathedrals, 2001*

Portfolio XIX: *Sandstone Country, 2002*

Portfolio XX: *Abstraction, 2003*

Portfolio XXI: *Alps, 2004*

Portfolio XXII: *Aegean Light, 2005*

This catalog was designed by Lynn Hoppel
and edited by Mary Beth Hinton.